A Woman's Guide to Low Self-Esteem

by Darlene Lacey

DM
DINER MIGHTY
GRAPHICS

BOOKS THAT SATISFY THE RAVENOUS READER
www.DinerMighty.com

This book is published as a work of satire. The author does not endorse nor promote any of the exercises, diets, products, personalities, or regimens mentioned in this book and does not present herself as an authority on women's health issues. Always consult a certified physician prior to beginning any diet or exercise routine. Images in this book come from the author's private collection or public domain sources and are considered fair use. If there have been any inadvertent copyright omissions, these can be corrected in future editions. Many of the images used in this book have been digitally cleaned, beautified, and/or simplified for design purposes without altering the original intent.

Bibliography:
Cellulite: Those Lumps, Bumps, and Bulges You Couldn't Lose Before by Nicole Ronsard
Gentlemen Prefer Blondes and *But Gentlemen Marry Brunettes* by Anita Loos
Glorify Yourself by Eleanore King
"How to Have a Full Bust" by Bettina Van Ness in *Home Needlework Magazine*
Nostrums and Quackery, Volume II by Arthur J. Cramp, M.D.
"The Woman with Two Chins" by Madame Julie D'Arcy

Special thanks to Grandma, who never had a positive thing to say about my appearance.

Print and electronic versions of this book designed by Diner Mighty Graphics, Los Angeles, Calif., U.S.A. Cover art and select interior illustrations by Joe Lacey.

Published by Diner Mighty Graphics, publisher of humor and pop culture books. DinerMighty.com

Diner Mighty Graphics and the DM graphics logo are trademarks of Diner Mighty.

ISBN: 978-1-7339842-5-6

Also available as a Kindle e-book

First Edition

Dedicated to
My Thighs

*"There is no exquisite beauty without some
strangeness in the proportion."*
~ Edgar Allan Poe

Table of Contents

Introduction

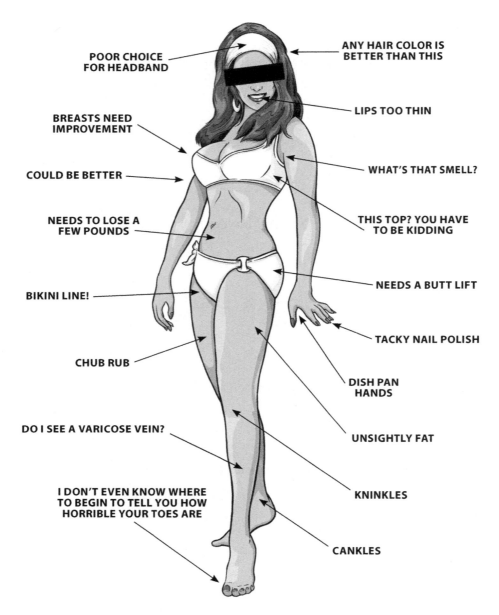

POOR CHOICE
FOR HEADBAND

ANY HAIR COLOR IS
BETTER THAN THIS

LIPS TOO THIN

BREASTS NEED
IMPROVEMENT

WHAT'S THAT SMELL?

COULD BE BETTER

THIS TOP? YOU HAVE
TO BE KIDDING

NEEDS TO LOSE A
FEW POUNDS

NEEDS A BUTT LIFT

BIKINI LINE!

TACKY NAIL POLISH

CHUB RUB

DISH PAN
HANDS

DO I SEE A VARICOSE VEIN?

UNSIGHTLY FAT

I DON'T EVEN KNOW WHERE
TO BEGIN TO TELL YOU HOW
HORRIBLE YOUR TOES ARE

KNINKLES

CANKLES

There's a saying that when we don't learn from the past we are doomed to repeat it. As time and technology move forward, it's easy to assume that society's views are also advancing brightly along. And this is true in some cases. In others, it is not. In the case of women's advertising, you might be surprised to learn that the minds of generations of women have been spinning on a carousel fueled by the same products, promises, and put-downs for over 100 years. These once blatantly negative messages have become more refined over the decades, but their essence remains. These messages have set up residence in women's minds and have been handed down as truisms, leaving even many empowered women today with low self-esteem. Hate your hair? Hate your knees? Hate your nose? Have you ever asked yourself *why?*

I wrote this book to answer that question, to provide the "smoking gun" that reveals how these ideas got trapped in our collective minds to begin with. A casual observation by my husband inspired me to write this. As he flipped through one of the many vintage women's magazines I love to collect, he remarked:

> "I can see why women could get paranoid about their appearance. Look at these ads — *you just can't win!*"

He showed me ad after ad filling the back pages: "Don't be FAT!" "Don't be SKINNY!" "Too tall?" "Too short?" "Thick legs?" "Thin legs?" "Scalp ODOR?" "Ashamed of your bust?" "Flatten your tummy!" "Remove ugly hair!" "Bleach those horrid age spots!" "Make skin look young again!" "IMPROVE YOUR FIGURE!" There was even an ad to cure stammering. *Well, who wouldn't stammer after all this!*

"Yes, *yes!*" I said excitedly, feeling vindicated. "These are the ads I grew up with. They look like a joke now, but they didn't back then. And it wasn't just magazines — books, newspapers, TV talk shows, and commercials bombarded women with checklists of flaws and how to correct them!"

This conversation got me wondering… these days, have we *truly* bought into the idea that we are all perfect and beautiful just the way we are? There's a lot of talk about it, but how many of us believe it deep down? How easy is it to shed our perceptions of ourselves when we have been fed a steady diet of messages about how we could and *should* be better? And if we're not, we only have ourselves to blame.

But that's not fair! I decided to grit my teeth, hold my nose, and do my best to hang onto my ego as I embarked on a quest to find out exactly **what** women have been exposed to over the decades. After scouring thousands of ads and articles, guess what I found? Even our great-great grandmothers were chastised constantly about their bust, their hair, their skin, their smell, their manners — *everything imaginable!* The fashions have changed, but the messages have not. They just come wrapped in a modern package. Are you struggling to meet today's fashion norms? Well, this is nothing new.

——FAMILY TREE – 1900s TO TODAY——

When I run a quick self-inspection, I can easily tally up eight things about myself that I have hated my whole life and at least twelve when I add new "flaws" that have come with getting older. The sad thing about this is that other people see me as totally fine. I think most women have had this experience. Complain about your looks, and you receive a chorus of sincere replies from friends of *"What?! You're **beautiful!**"*

What's your story? Measure your self-esteem by rating how you disagree or agree with the following statements. We'll check back in on you at the conclusion of this journey through the Land of Low Self-Esteem.

Self-Esteem Pre-Survey	Strongly Disagree 1	Disagree 2	Neutral 3	Agree 4	Strongly Agree 5
I would like to change the size or shape of my bust.					
I would like to change at least one thing about my face.					
I'm horrified if someone catches a whiff of my body odor.					
I would like to lose or gain some weight.					
I would like to change at least one thing about my arms and/or legs.					
Growing old terrifies me.					
My rear end could be a lot better.					

Low self-esteem is a sensitive subject, so I decided to take a lighthearted look at it. Why shed tears when we can laugh? And although I am leading you along this trek through pop history, I don't want the lens to be limited to my own. For this reason, I have recruited a team of experts to weigh in on topics. *Meet the team!*

I have also recruited a top advice columnist on beauty, poise, and charm. Allow me introduce Mrs. Etta Kitt.

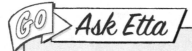

Greetings, Dear Readers:
I am much better than you. How, exactly?
You shall soon find out.

In closing, I want to acknowledge that there's nothing wrong with self-improvement. If we want to change something about ourselves, why not! It's a personal choice. It is wise, however, to use some skepticism when deciding how and why you are going to do it. This book's purpose is to not serve as an authority on the efficacy of products and services — its purpose is to reveal how advertising has shaped our view of ourselves.

Before we embark on this journey, I leave you with the most perfect woman from 1916. See you how compare.

Enjoy the hard facts of life!
~Darlene

Diet and Exercise the Secret, She Says.

AMERICA'S NEWEST VENUS.
Nana Sterling Beats the Venus of Milo by 14 Points in the Percentage of Physical Perfection

Nana Sterling eats only two meals a day. The first comes usually between the hours of 10 and 11; the second sharp at 5.

MISS NANA STERLING
"America's most perfect woman."

Cold water keeps the fat out of your tissues.

Walks at least five miles a day, one before breakfast.

Can play tennis and basketball as well as most girls.

Fine for the figure, this little exercise stunt night and morning.

NANA STERLING'S MEASUREMENTS
Which won her the medal for the nearest approach to a perfect physique to be found among the women of the United States.

Age — 19 years.	Weight — 130 pounds.
Height — 5 feet 6 inches.	Chest — 35 inches.
Neck — 13 inches.	Waist — 26 inches.
Bust — 38 inches.	Thigh — 22 inches.
Hips — 38 inches.	Arm — 11 inches.
Calf — 14 inches.	Wrist — 6¼ inches.
Forearm — 10 inches.	

It's What's Up Front that Counts!

Size Matters

Let's begin by getting a touchy topic off our chest: the bosom, breasts, boobs, melons, jugs… whatever you care to call them. They come in so many shapes and sizes that poets and plastic surgeons can barely keep up: large, small, firm, saggy, full, flat, round, pointed, pert, pendulous, symmetrical, cockeyed, ripe, overripe… the list goes on. And, for every word that describes them, there are ten slang names for them. Why? Because everywhere we go, there they are, and most of the time, they get there first.

When I was a girl awaiting the moment to buy a training bra, there was a lot of playground buzz about who got hers and who was still waiting. Boys would snap the girls' bra straps, laugh, and run away. It wasn't clear whether they trying to tease these girls, get their attention, or both, but one thing was clear — it was a big deal. Rumor was that once you got them, you would be on your way to fabulous dates and dances. But what if you didn't? Until you did there was always the fear that the Boobs Fairy might pass you by. It happened in my family for at least two generations.

So, the worry begins at an early age that whatever you have may not be good enough. But why? Ask a guy how many pictures of topless women he could look at until he got bored, and he'll reply, "How many are there?" Considering how much they are stared at and longed for by their fans, it seems any pair will do. But it's hard to shake the feeling that they could be… well… **better**. How the heck did we get that idea in our heads? *I wonder….*

Shape Me, Shake Me, Squeeze Me

For more than the last 100 years, women have been bombarded with ads for products with big promises of how they can obtain the "ideal bosom." I've been hearing about it my entire life. My P.E. teachers even led the girls in exercise to the chant: *We must! We must! We must increase our bust!*

Experiences such as these lead the mind down a path: a woman's work is never done when it comes to keeping up appearances. But what is the ideal bosom? Bustline fashion trends have come and gone, sometimes glorifying the trim forms of the flappers and flat-chested icon, Twiggy, then celebrating the voluptuous curves of stars such as Sophia Loren and Beyonce. So, does anything go?

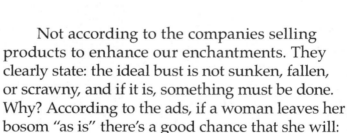

DEVELOP A LOVELY

FULLER BOSOM

Become **DESIROUS** — enjoy new Romantic Triumphs! Be enticingly feminine!

Highly **SUCCESSFUL** method. Home course for Bust Development —takes only few minutes a day!

If LOVE is missing from your life, you may be helped through this simple photo-instruction method, which shows you how to apply the prescribed techniques, in the privacy of your own home. Easy to follow, 64 pages, all fully illustrated — for WOMEN ONLY.

Don't let skepticism delay or deny you this opportunity for NEW happiness! GUARANTEED — If after 30 days you are not satisfied, for any reason, return this course for a complete refund. Fill in coupon below, and mail with $2. Course will be mailed to you in plain wrapper.

INTIMATE BOOKS CO., Dept. 1032
125 E 46th St., New York 17, N.Y.
Please send me BONOMO RITUAL in plain wrapper. I am enclosing check, M. O. for $2. If I am not satisfied, my money to be refunded in full, under your 30-day guarantee.
NAME ENID LITTLE
Print Clearly
ADDRESS APT. 24A WALL STREET
CITY SUNKEN HILLS ZONE 8

Not according to the companies selling products to enhance our enchantments. They clearly state: the ideal bust is not sunken, fallen, or scrawny, and if it is, something must be done. Why? According to the ads, if a woman leaves her bosom "as is" there's a good chance that she will:

a.) never find love
b.) lose her love
 and/or
c.) miss her one and only opportunity to be the sumptuous goddess she was always meant to be, if only she had wised up and sent away for help.

Man, as I kept going deeper researching this topic, I really started to sweat! Where does happiness begin and where does it end? I always thought life choices were the backbone of one's destiny, but could it be that genetics combined with a sluggardly attitude toward self-improvement have been charting our courses all along?

Looking at the ads alone was bad enough, but then I started to notice patterns in the juxtaposition of the ads with other ads. Might there even be a connection between a beautiful bust and prosperity? Let's hope this is just an unfortunate coincidence!

Shape Up With Beauty Bells

Enjoy figure loveliness, a high beautiful bust, graceful posture, all yours using BEAUTY BELLS. Remove inches from waist, hips, thighs. You can add or take off where it counts with this scientific contouring method. Thrilling results in just one week. Satisfaction guaranteed. Order today this pair of elegantly fashioned Beauty Bells, 4 lbs. each, complete with foot straps and illustrated booklet. Post PPD, $8.95. Send check or M.O. to Randia Co., P.O. Box 752, Venice, Calif.

Borrow $107 to $1212 By Mail

Only 24 payments of $62 a month repays $1212. Borrow entirely by mail. Pay off all your debts . . . only one small monthly payment instead of many. Completely confidential. No endorsers. No embarrassing investigations. Over 60 years of service. Try us. Write for FREE loan papers, including loan application and full details. Postal Finance Company, Dept. 171CB, 817 East Colorado Blvd., Pasadena, California, 91101.

Let's forget about finances. Could there truly be a connection between one's bustline and romantic fulfillment? Let's check in with our resident expert on all things womanly, Mrs. Etta Kitt.

Go > Ask Etta

Dear Mrs. Kitt ~ I just don't get it. I'm nice, I'm smart, I earn good money, I'm dependable, I keep in shape, and I'm even a good cook. Yet, I can't find love! Can you explain this?

Sincerely,
Flat Out of Clues

Dear Flat:
It's your **bustline,** dear.
No one is interested in a sunken chest…
unless it's at the bottom of the sea!

Mrs. Kitt! How can you say that! All women are beautiful, right?
RIGHT?

Well then, **what to do?** I found a lot of options… exercises, vitamins, tablets, massage creams, diets, baths, vacuums, padded bras, push-up bras, pump-up bras, water bras… what to choose? Let's break it down.

ISOMETRIC EXERCISE — Just grab a book and you are ready to start the isometric bust developing exercise.

Better Safe than Sorry

Some "get big fast" schemes have been quite benign. There is the fitness option with upper body exercises. Push-ups, arm circles, dumbbell flies, and isometrics have all been hailed as effective as long as a woman sticks with the program. Nothing wrong with getting strong and fit; it's just unfortunate that the main motivator for doing it is to get a perfect bosom as opposed to, say, enjoying better health with improved posture, defending oneself, or opening that stupid pickle jar.

Padded, push-up, or even inflatable bras have been another harmless way to add some shape to one's liking. Again, nothing really wrong with this, except that the ads for them have often come with some unwanted connotations. They seem to be a dirty secret, best worn with anonymity. They also seem to be a key to social charm. Apparently, with the right padded bra at a party, you can let the bra do the talking!

"Miss Personality" Padded Bra

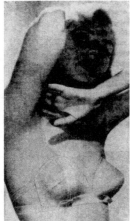
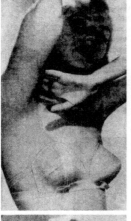

Every Breath You Take

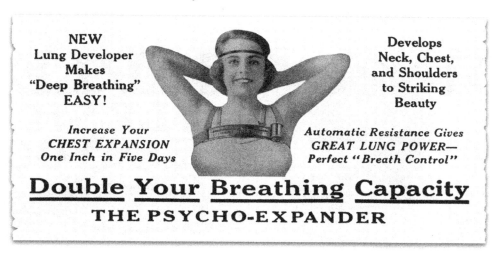

NEW
Lung Developer
Makes
"Deep Breathing"
EASY!

Develops
Neck, Chest,
and Shoulders
to Striking
Beauty

Increase Your
CHEST EXPANSION
One Inch in Five Days

Automatic Resistance Gives
GREAT LUNG POWER—
Perfect "Breath Control"

Double Your Breathing Capacity
THE PSYCHO-EXPANDER

Deep breathing has been another seemingly benign and simple method touted to make oneself more titillating. In 1910, one beauty advice columnist took this concept to another level by disclosing the little-known fact that playing the trumpet could transform you into a crumpet. According to "How to Have a Full Bust" by Bettina Van Ness in *Home Needlework Magazine*:

Another good developing exercise is to blow a horn for ten minutes daily. If you take good deep breaths, as I want you to, you will make a great deal of noise and alienate your family, but be a martyr in a good cause. When your family sees you blossoming out like a rose they will bless the obnoxious horn-blowing. Let that thought be your consolation in times of trial.

Perhaps deep breathing is not so benign after all. Ask the poor husband of the woman who followed this advice.

Flesh for Fantasy

Back in the "good old days" (the early 1900s) the "scientific breakthrough" of **Dr. Charles Flesh Food** (yes, Dr. Charles Flesh Food) provided a means for how a "handsome woman may preserve her charms and her plain angular sister attain a fine complexion and a rounded figure". In an ad from 1906, women were advised:

> *It is certain that the Dr. Charles Flesh Food can restore the fallen, shrunken or immature bosom to the rounded proportions of the perfect bust. It has never failed, when its use has been persistent, and the prescribed directions followed. An imperfect bust development is unfortunate.*

What was Dr. Charles Flesh Food? According to one of my favorite books, *Nostrums and Quackery, Volume II* (1921), a compilation of findings from *The Journal of the American Medical Association* by Arthur J. Cramp, M.D., it was a "highly perfumed pink ointment" made up mostly of Vaseline and starch. According to their lab report, what it "lacked in therapeutic efficiency, it made up for in color and odor." *Ew!* Imagine the poor woman rubbing it on diligently every day. Now, imagine her following it up by blaring a horn for ten minutes. Now, let's hope there is a potion for wiping this sad image out of our minds.

But Wait a Minute...

How did we get off on this tangent that somehow breast enlargement is the path to the "ideal bosom"? Aren't our differences what makes each of us special? Didn't I once hear someone say that? I'm pretty sure I did!

Well, despite all this and regardless of the careful choice of words in advertisements throughout the years, the objective that society has dealt us has been pretty clear:

big boobs or bust!

The Way to Eden

I know what some of you are thinking: *Dr. Charles Flesh Food? What dizzy dame would fall for that? We have evolved so much since the primitive days of 1906! Besides, Dr. Cramp blew the lid off that scheme! Surely, we all learned from this.*

Well, think again. Promises of bigger bosoms became even bigger business as the decades wore on. In 1959, U.S. Postmaster General Arthur E. Summerfield disclosed that mail order medical frauds such as the "Lady Ample Bust Developer" robbed the gullible public of at least $50 million annually.

THROUGHOUT AMERICA WOMEN ARE REPORTING
Amazing Gains on their Bustlines
by using the
FABULOUS *Mark Eden Developer*

BEFORE her Mark Eden Course
BUST: 34A

AFTER her Mark Eden Course
BUST: 36C

In the 1960s, advertisements for the Mark Eden Bust Developer featuring voluptuous women began casting a long shadow all over magazines and newspapers. For over a decade the U.S. Postal Service and the Federal Trade Commission tried to bust Mark Eden on the basis of fraud.

The Mark Eden ads included testimonials from women claiming to have gained three to four inches in their bustline in a matter of weeks. The keyword here was "bustline" since the Mark Eden Developer developed, if anything, muscle. It was a clam-shaped device with two plastic pieces attached by a steel spring. Women were supposed to use its dynamic tension every day in order to expand that bustline.

MARK EDEN IS THE WORLD'S MOST SUCCESSFUL BUSTLINE DEVELOPER

"I increased my _Bustline_ from _36" to a Full 40"_ _in just 6 weeks_
with the Mark Eden Developer"

Unfortunately for the FTC, a test done at the University of California showed that the participants' chests did in fact increase in measurement by 2–3 inches in the first few weeks. Buoyed by this victory and steady profits, the Mark Eden empire continued to expand, offering a wide variety of body-altering products such as the Astro-Trimmer (a band worn around the waist) and Slim Skins (sauna pants attached to a vacuum cleaner). Eventually a second university study, this time commissioned by the Postal Service, deemed these products worthless and in 1983 Eileen and Jack Feather, the California couple responsible for this juggernaut, were indicted on 11 counts of mail fraud. They wound up paying the U.S. Postal Service $1.1 million, stopped selling these products as part of a settlement, and closed up shop.

Sandra Wilder
before her
Mark Eden Course
BUST 36"

Sandra Wilder today ~ A Full 41"

So… If We Have Learned Nothing… What Have We Learned?

Well, to be honest, I'm not really sure. The Quest for the Perfect Breast seems to be one that will never end. My takeaway from my research is that breast augmentation is not unlike splitting the atom — it can be attempted, but it probably won't be achieved at home. As with most anything, you can make some changes on your own, but these days many women opt for surgical procedures. Of course, these cost a fair amount of money, and risks come with any surgical procedure, but it appears as though there are many women who pursued their dream and happily fulfilled it. And maybe there really are women who have always loved their bosom just the way it is. Just ask Mrs. Etta Kitt.

— Or don't.

Let's Face It—
You're Flawed

Why the Long Face?

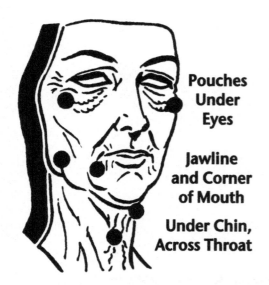

Pouches Under Eyes

Jawline and Corner of Mouth

Under Chin, Across Throat

This is a long chapter for what seems to be a simple topic, but a woman's face is such a complex thing. There's the shape of the face, the proportions, and the skin, eyes, nose, ears, mouth, and chin. Then, there are the sub-details: the eyebrows, eyelashes, lips, teeth, acne, wrinkles, sagging, and what they say about you as a person. The face is a place where anything that can go wrong probably will go wrong. That's a whole world of worry for a woman to face!

HORRIFYING QUOTE ABOUT FACIAL BEAUTY #1

Your face is your personal flag... and it's always on parade! How do you carry your banner — proudly and handsomely, or does it droop and sag in mournful display?

~Ad for a 1950s facial beauty system

To add to this worry, who the heck even knows what's going on when you're without the benefit of a mirror? You leave the house looking perfect, only to find a big smear of lipstick on your teeth when you come home. Then, there is the horrific variable of lighting. You look fantastic at home, but when you primp in the powder room mirror at a store, you find a sad old bag staring back at you.

I've heard that photos don't lie, but what is the truth when you look gorgeous in one photo and like a sub-human in a photo shared by a friend who happens to look flawless in it? That's why many women prefer selfies. We can use filters to create larger eyes, smoother skin, tapered jawlines, and gleaming teeth… a woman can post fifty selfies and look like a different person in each one. Would we recognize each other if we met in real life?

What matters more? How you see yourself (as expressed in your selfie) or how others see you? And how *do* they see you? No one is ever going to tell you the truth.

Meanwhile, there are plenty of companies out there who want you to believe this: *that face of yours could use some work!* Let me guide you through this blemished tale. To help keep track, I've created a checklist of details to fret over. *Rate yourself as we go along!*

HORRIFYING QUOTE ABOUT FACIAL BEAUTY #2

Many women powder their faces before a dressing table equipped with electric lights and go blithely forth into the sunshine thinking to make a fine effect. Instead, they look more like whitewashed clowns made up to go in the circus ring.

~Advice column on how to powder your nose, 1919

Doomed from Birth

FACE SHAPE	
☐ Oval	☐ Not Oval
○ I am perfect!	○ Round ○ Square ○ Pear ○ Long ○ Heart ○ Diamond ○ Nothing that can be described with one word

Let's start with the face as a whole. If it's true that nobody's perfect, why do we keep trying? Over the decades, diagrams, T-squares, and micrometers have been deployed to determine facial perfection. Why? To find the woman with the perfect face.

(*Spoiler alert — it's not you!*)

I grew up reading about how the oval face was the perfect face. Sorry everyone — not the round, square, pear, long, heart, or diamond. The **oval** face.

If you weren't blessed with an oval face, plenty of workarounds have been provided to give your misshapen lump the illusion of perfection. Hairstyle tricks, makeup tricks, jewelry tricks, glasses tricks, and stylish hat tricks will save you. These might fool the gullible public, but you know the truth that lurks beneath them.

I tried to analyze my face shape when I was young, but I never felt sure — it was an ovalish-squarish-roundish thing. I decided to think of it as oval. That simplified things. Truth be told, though, mine falls into the category of "nothing that can be described with one word," and from what I have read, most women's do too.

One might think that at least the oval-faced woman could feel good about herself. Unfortunately, this is only one facet of the Rubik's Cube of facial perfection.

Guide to Glamor in Glasses

Face Shape	Beauty Aims	Recommended Style
SQUARE	Reduce overall facial squareness, soften lines.	
ROUND	Narrow the appearance of the face. Minimize round look.	
TRIANGULAR	Increase width of narrow forehead. Minimize wide chin line.	
OVAL	Ideal facial type. Frame should not distort shape.	
DIAMOND	Increase width of narrow forehead, minimize cheekbones.	
HEART	Minimize forehead and cheekbones, widen chin line.	
OBLONG	Reduce length of face.	

Do the Math

FACIAL PROPORTIONS		
☐ **Golden Ratio**	☐ **Everyone Else**	
○ Again, I am perfect!	○ Things that can be corrected with makeup	○ Things that can't

Another old saying is "beauty is in the eye of the beholder." This seems believable, but ads will tell you that it's not subjective. Math has been used as a way to quantify facial beauty for decades. In 1912, some dark-hearted soul invented the Kallometer. It was a frame you held up to your face to find out how your proportions rated in terms of a beauty ideal.

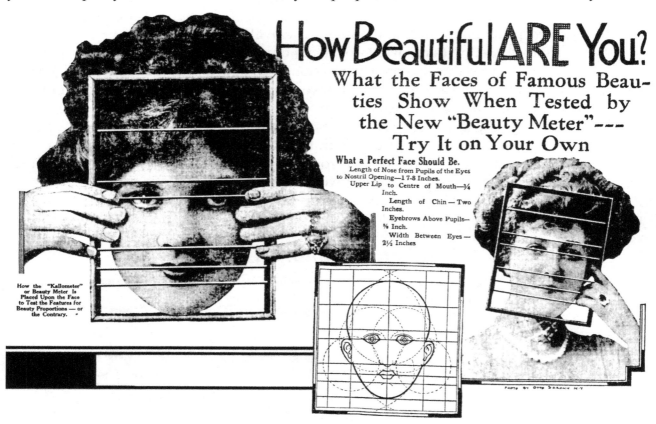

If you didn't want to spring for a Kallometer, you could use the handy measurements in the ad. Who's ready to try this out? I made a feeble attempt but could not read fractions of inches while squinting in the mirror.

What a Perfect Face Should Be

✓ Length of Nose from Pupils of the Eyes to Nostril Opening — 1⅞ Inches.
✓ Upper Lip to Center of Mouth — ¾ Inch.
✓ Length of Chin — 2 Inches.
✓ Eyebrows Above Pupils — ⅝ Inch.
✓ Width Between Eyes — 2½ Inches.

In the 1920s, movie director Allan Dwan, a once-professor of engineering, determined the mathematical criteria for a "movie face":

Charting the Movie Face

The Perfect Screen Beauty Must Possess Features Standardized and Mathematically Proportioned According to Rules Fixed by a Scientific Movie Director!

1. *The lines of the prettiest chin must form an obtuse angle.*

2. *The mouth when smiling should be a fifth larger than when in repose.*

3. *From ear to ear must equal the distance from chin to crown.*

4. *The eyes must be apart the distance of one eye width.*

But wait—! In 1933, eminent portrait painter, Penrhyn Stanlaws, asserted that there was not a single perfect screen beauty among Hollywood's stars. Citing some examples, he said:

> **Katharine Hepburn** — *"Her chin and the lower part of her face project too far. Anthropologists have a name for such a facial type: they call it prognathic. Artists call it 'horsy.'"*

> **Greta Garbo** — *"She has a sleepy, sophisticated look, attained by deep eye sockets and a peculiar slant of the upper lip. These are not aids to beauty."*

Oh, man! ***Good thing he wasn't around when I was born!***

Well, all this was coming from Hollywood, and we all understand that screen stars have always been held up to a higher standard than the rest of us slobs. But are they? Or have the stars just been sacrificed to serve as a cautionary tale for the rest of us to step up our game? After all, scientific studies have shown that even newborn babies prefer to gaze longer at faces that adults rated as attractive. If this is something hardwired into humans, are less-than-perfect women eternally doomed to fight for the leftovers in the romantic banquet of life?

These days, the "golden ratio" is a popular mathematical way to judge facial beauty. It involves dividing the face horizontally into thirds based on the eyes and the mouth, then vertically dividing it from the inner eye to the outside edge of the face, then subdividing that section from the outer eye to the edge of the face, and on and on it goes. Who has time for all this? *Who do you think!* **Women!**

Betty Compson Has Been Selected as Combining All That Is Desirable in Vivid Beauty for the Camera.

As the Dotted Lines Indicate the Proportions of the Head and Features of Mae Marsh Were Subjected to a Right Mathematical Computation.

Beauty Is Actually Skin Deep

SKIN			
☐ **Flawless**	☐ **Flawed**		
○ Don't hate me because I'm beautiful.	**Blemishes** ○ Pimples ○ Blackheads	**Facial Lines** ○ Frown lines ○ Old lady wrinkles	**Skin Tone** ○ Sagging ○ Crepey

What if you are fortunate enough to have a face that achieves mathematical perfection? Don't think you can rest on your laurels. Do you frown? Stay up late dancing? Smoke cigars? Eat half a pizza? Any or all of these behaviors could put you in need of a good face concealer.

FACIAL FLAWS?

1. FROWN LINES
2. UNDER EYE CIRCLES
3. FACIAL LINES
4. BLEMISHES

Sally Hansen 'undercover'

It's fair to say that we women are merely enhancing our natural beauty by using any and all products and procedures there are to make the most of it. However, spending each day scrutinizing "facial flaws" and applying soap, medicine, make-up and moisturizer to fight them takes a toll on one's self-esteem. It's easy to start thinking that everybody has nicer skin than you. Maybe it's true, or maybe you just haven't scrutinized your friends under a microscope.

I consulted my facial beauty expert to share her secret to a flawless complexion:

> ## Expert Advice
>
> *A little sleep, healthy living, and soap and water is sometimes all that's needed to brighten your face and give it a marvelous dewy look.*
>
> *If that doesn't work — **spackle over it!***

I could go on and on about how ads tell us that young skin, old skin, oily skin, dry skin, and even acid skin can ruin an otherwise splendid face. The desire for facial skin beauty could even lead a woman to drastic measures — *like applying a laxative to her face!* Sad to think that both ends of a woman might require the same treatment. Is there any human dignity left in this world?

TWO REMARKABLE New-Type CREAMS!

with a special beauty-giving ingredient
MILK OF MAGNESIA

PHILLIPS · PHILLIPS

If Your Problem is PIMPLES and You Are Doing THIS.... *for Pete's Sake STOP!*

Stop Squeezing Pimples and Spreading Infection!

Stop Looking Like a Painted Doll Trying to Hide Pimples!

Stop Sealing in Pimple Germs With Heavy Creams, Greases, or Powders!

Stop Being a Lonesome Hermit Waiting for Pimples to Disappear!

Acne and blackheads are timeless foes of feminine perfection, especially when we are young. As the years grind on, these oily nuisances usually diminish and become replaced with a worse enemy, sagging and wrinkled skin. It's often the case that we are so busy fixing "flaws" in our twenties and thirties that we don't realize until we're older how good our skin looked. By that time, it's too late to bask in the beauty of youth. All we're left with is the bittersweet sharing of old photos and having friends exclaim: "Beautiful! Is that *you?*"

THE FACIAL BEAUTY TIMELINE OF TERROR!

ADOLESCENCE
The freak show begins!

TEEN AGE
Desperate to escape greasy disfigurement!

MATURITY
Visions of death masks haunt the mind!

MIDDLE AGE
Desperate to recapture greasy disfigured youth!

The Eyes Don't Have It

EYES			
☐ **Vivacious / Stunning**	☐ **Need Work**		
○ Yes, everyone tells me this!	**Eyebrows** ○ Too thick ○ Too thin ○ Nonexistent	**Eye Lashes** ○ Never enough	**Eye Makeup** ○ Too thick ○ Too thin ○ Nonexistent ○ Misguided

Am I all alone in wishing I had better eyes? Until writing this book, I thought I was. The world is full of women with beautiful eyes completely unlike mine — large with heavy lids, thick lashes, and eyebrows set high and far apart. But then I used my sad little eyes to read between the lines, and I realized that the eye beauty industry has convinced women that every woman's eyes need some enhancement. How many women will even leave the house or allow their picture to be taken without eye makeup?

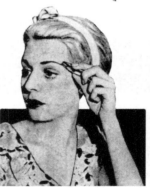

It's no wonder we've become so insecure about this. We've been told our entire lives that whatever we're doing… no. Just **no**. Plain eyes don't cut it. Eyes must be flirtier, more dramatic, more alluring. Lashes must be longer and thicker. Makeup is either too heavy or too light, and it needs to change with the setting and the season.

Eyebrows are particularly vulnerable to low self-esteem. At times, fashion dictates that they be thick; other times, thin. Shave them for fashion, and you risk never seeing them again. Tattoo or microblade them, and you risk having brows you hate for years. Despite these risks, we can't leave our brows alone.

The bottom line: even if you have a makeup look that works, it will become dated in three months. What if you choose not to wear it? This will reflect an "uninteresting personality." And here I was thinking that my Miss Personality padded bra was all I needed.

BEFORE
Without proper makeup, eyes are lustreless—reflecting an uninteresting personality.

AFTER
Wide-awake and glowing beauty resulted from the use of proper technique and cosmetics

One good thing about eye makeup is that even if you fail with it one day, you can wipe it off and try again the next day. Unfortunately, eye color is another story. Over the decades, love-smitten balladeers have gushed over blue-eyed beauties. Not the most welcome sentiment for the 70–90 percent of the population with brown eyes. Surveys show blue eyes usually coming in first as most attractive, with green sometimes edging out blue. One thing is for certain — when it comes to what we see and hear in the media, brown eyes are **never** number one, so if you have them? You lose. Forever.

…Or do you? For decades, science has been striving to let us to have the color of our choice. Tinted contact lenses are one strategy, and laser treatments can remove the melanin pigment that darkens one's eyes. Iris implant surgery is even available in some countries. It seems that we have become convinced that a change in eye color equates to a change for the better in our lives.

Women also go to extreme measures for large eyes. Some wear circle contact lenses and heavy makeup to create "dolly eyes," bright enormous eyes like those seen in anime and manga. Some also opt for blepharoplasty, a cosmetic procedure to make their eyes larger and rounder.

Looking for a less drastic way to enlarge your eyes? Here's a home remedy offered up by famed beauty Gaby Deslys in 1911. Her advice? Train yourself to keep your eyes open! Otherwise, your eyelids will half close, grow heavy, and your eyes will look about half their natural size. To quote:

I WILL my eyes to be wide open, to look animated and pleasant, though they could often look as bored as those of other people I see among the passers-by.

Need motivation to make a practice of this? She adds:

Someone told me the eye was the shop window of the soul. All I can say is that the windows are often badly trimmed with the oldest, stupidest wares, and would not tempt me, at least, to explore the rest of the store.

Okay, I'm in! If you run into me and see me staring, you'll know why.

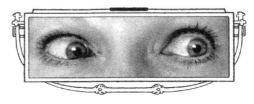

Too Bad about that Nose

NOSE			
☐ Poetry	**☐ Needs Work**		
○ I think that I shall never see a nose as lovely as the one on me.	○ Long ○ Bulbous	○ Bumpy	○ Fat
	○ Angular ○ Flaring	○ Narrow	○ Round

Your Trouble May Be as Plain as the Nose on Your Face

The author of a 1961 article stated that vanity was not the only reason why 30–50,000 rhinoplasties were being performed each year with 16- to 19-year-old girls the largest group of patients. The author explained that "few people can avoid emotional trauma if they have a deformity which is as impossible to conceal as a nose." Seems fair, but what is a "deformity"? The author went on to provide a case study about a miserable teenage girl who inherited her father's big nose. I guess in some cases looking like Dad qualifies as a deformity!

What is the ideal nose? The "Greek nose" or "straight nose" has been cited throughout the decades as perfect. It features a straight bridge with no bumps or turns and protrudes at a 106-degree angle between the forehead and the lips. Grab those geometry class tools again, ladies! I'm not going to bother because I can tell you with no measuring that mine is not this. I've read that only three percent of the population has one, and I am not that special.

According to industry statistics, the number of nose jobs has been whittling down since the start of the 21st century, but still close to a million people, mostly women, opt for one. How much of this is driven by personal desire and how much by social pressure? Once, I saw an Ear Nose Throat doctor for an ear problem. As he worked on my ear, he scowled critically at my nose and asked whether I had considered cosmetic surgery. I said the thought had never crossed my mind. He replied, "Maybe it *should*." I never went back. I like my nose, despite inheriting it from my mother and grandmother who hated theirs.

The author of a newspaper column from 1889 saw the bright side in women who lacked the Grecian ideal of a nose:

The woman with a crooked nose is usually more fortunate in friendships, as she is less likely to be scornful of those less pleasantly situated than herself. […] The same nose will be more patient in planning and awaiting results in life. In love affairs patient, possibly because its wearer is not accustomed to the prompt capitulation of the lovers of the Greek-nosed maiden.

Yikes! Who has the name of a good plastic surgeon?

Perfection

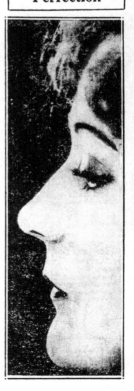

Despite advances in surgical techniques, having a nose job is still not a trivial procedure. It costs thousands of dollars and there's no guarantee that you will be happy with the result.

In closing, I leave you with one more quote I ran across in my research. No wonder so many women feel they are just a nose job away from happiness!

HORRIFYING QUOTE ABOUT FACIAL BEAUTY #3

Among the things which must be accepted as unalterable is the shape of the nose. [...] The nose is the most prominent feature of the human countenance, and it has a great deal to do with beauty or ugliness. [...] Unfortunately, also, the ugliness of an ugly nose can never be redeemed by 'expression.' As a popular writer has said, "The plain mouth may break into a smile to touch the coldest heart with a gleam of sympathetic joy; the dullest eyes may light up with a radiance wholly unlooked for," but there is no hope of an ugly nose being modified in this way. Nor is there any possibility of hiding or disguising this unfortunate member if one would wish to do so. It stands in the center of the face 'like a lighthouse on a rocky coast,' the cynosure of all eyes. The only way of dealing with it is to accept it.

~Newspaper column about facial beauty, 1882

New Noses Made Out Of Flesh And Bone

How the Plastic Surgeon Moulds Them in Any Desired Shape or Size and Makes Them as Durable and Efficient as the Original Ones

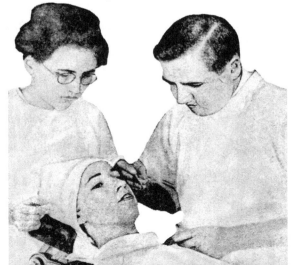

Turn that Frown Upside Down

MOUTH		
☐ **Enchanting**	☐ **Needs Work**	
○ My smile makes everyone happy!	**Teeth** ○ Dingy ○ Yellow ○ Crooked ○ Gone	**Lips** ○ Too Thick ○ Too Thin ○ Too Thick *and* Too Thin

We learned in "Horrifying Quote about Facial Beauty #3" that a plain mouth may be redeemed by "expression," but what if that smile somehow makes everything worse? And you're the last to know?

With the high price of dentistry, sometimes it feels like a victory to merely still have teeth in one's head. Sadly, I have learned from ads there are two kinds of teeth: "teeth for getting fabulous dinner dates" and "teeth for chewing dry toast at home alone." Now you know too.

THEY CALLED HER "HORSE-TOOTH" HELEN UNTIL-

Even if you have white teeth, what about those lips? Too thin? Too thick? Thin on top, but thick on the bottom or vice versa? Smoker's lines and wrinkles? Loose lips might sink ships, but they are the least of women's problems. Lip injections and filler injections are a solution; makeup techniques are another. Creams can also be applied. There is no permanent solution, not even lip liner tattoos, due to the ever-changing nature of one's lips. And I think we have all seen that too much tampering with lips over time is not a good thing!

THIN LIPS
Build up the lipline above the natural line with an undercoat of a darker lipstick. Blend a lighter shade over it.

THICK LIPS
Make thinner by covering with foundation; then apply lipstick inside natural lipline. Concentrate color at the *center*.

Don't Be a Clown—Use Lipstick With Finesse

Lipstick is an easy way to spruce up one's lips, but is it foolproof? The answer is evident when one sees what happens when little girls and drunks apply it. Any beauty expert will tell you there's no wedding ring in a three-ring circus. A wise old clown once said, "If I were da Vinci, I wouldn't be juggling pies." Good advice, as we too must realize our artistic shortcomings as we struggle with lip liner and pots of lip gloss.

What's at stake if you can't master the fine art of pucker paint? Stolen kisses… snatched by your rival for your heart's desire.

Then again, maybe you seem to be doing everything right, but you're not getting to first base. Well, let me be frank. The problem? It lies elsewhere. It's your awful lipstick. There's no way every lipstick is going to give you "lovable lips." How will you know when you have them? Your date will take you in a mad embrace and tell you your lips look lovable. This is not rocket science! As usual, we only have our own ignorance and hubris to blame.

How Low Can You Go?

CHIN				
☐ **Firm / Pert**	☐ **Sad, Really**			
○ I love my life!	**Too Many** ○ Double ○ Triple ○ # ___	○ Sagging	○ Too Long	○ Too Short

Hey, readers, how's it going with the checklist by now? Have you gone this far with your self-esteem intact? Oval face, perfect facial proportions, luminous skin, dazzling eyes, Grecian nose, pearly teeth, kissable lips? If so, congratulations! Now… how about that chin? No big deal in the scheme of things, right?

> ## HORRIFYING QUOTE ABOUT FACIAL BEAUTY #4
>
> *A double chin costs a woman everything in the world worthwhile — romance, affection, comeliness, beauty — everything. No romance can survive a double chin.*
>
> ~Ad for double chin remedy, 1911

Fortunately, chin issues don't usually affect us until later in life, but they can strike at any age, and guess whose fault it is? Read this excerpt from the newspaper feature "The Woman with Two Chins" by Madame Julie D'Arcy.

> *"My face looks just like a pudding," said a pretty woman surveying herself in the glass, "and it's my own fault, too. I've been eating too much."*
>
> *The chafing dish will be the death of woman as far as her beauty is concerned. It tempts her evenings, and of all things in the world, there is nothing that puts flesh on you like eating at night.*
>
> *Thin women take notice. If you want to get fat, eat in the evening. Eat all of something you like very well. Then go to bed and sleep soundly until morning. You will awake with an extra layer of flesh right under your chin. Food eaten at night seems to settle there.*
>
> *And here is another point for the thin woman. Eat what you want. Nothing fattens you like eating the food you like. Fat women always eat what they want. If they cannot get it, they go without.*

Uh-oh! Well, what happens if and when I break down at some point in my life and eat something I like? What then? I'm really not sure I can postpone this forever! And I'm guessing you can't either.

Fortunately, there's a solution, a chin strap which can be worn reading, sleeping, and watching TV. Shouldn't bother anybody around the house, since the woman with the bad chin is surely living alone.

FIRM CHIN MUSCLES

Chin strap—helps firm THROAT and CHIN muscles, prevent sagging. Comfortable to wear while reading, sleeping, watching TV. Quality white elastic, adjustable strap. Only $1.00 (Add 35¢ post. and hand); 2 for $2.00 (Add 35¢ for post. and hand). Satisfaction guaranteed.

I also found a carefree exercise regimen that all of us could and should repeat as often as possible each day:

1. Drop your head back as far as you can and chew slowly for five minutes.

2. Roll your head around your shoulders, first five times clockwise and then five times anti-clockwise, stretching hard in every direction.

3. Whenever possible, alternately smile and purse the lips.

4. Carry your chin parallel to the floor at all times.

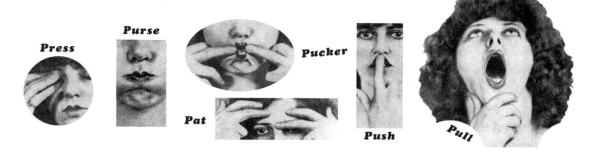

I found many more exercises and remedies for this social disaster waiting to happen, including surgical procedures such as liposuction, a technique that can also remove the dreaded "turkey gobbler" from one's neck. However, I'm going to spare us all by declaring the neck technically out of bounds for a chapter about the face. We have all suffered enough by now.

Go ▷ Ask Etta

Dear Mrs. Kitt ~ I am a professional model. I have a perfect face with flawless petal-soft skin, and I have appeared in numerous makeup commercials because of my flawless face. All my female friends envy me. So, why are all my dates "first dates"? Help! My biological clock is ticking!

Signed,
Bloom Will Soon Be Off the Rose

Dear Miss Bloom:
A rose by any name would —
Ahem! I am going to stop here and strongly advise you to turn to the next page.

I Hate to Break the News — But...

YOU STINK!

The Silent Offender

No one is *safe!*

Not just you, but everybody. As one ad grimly states: Policeman, 'phone operator,' housewife or millionaire – every one of us, no matter who we are, *may offend unknowingly.* *Yeeks!* That means me!

Another ad bluntly spells out the sad consequences if others catch a whiff of you:

People who offend are not wanted—
either as employees or friends.
You can readily appreciate why.

Yes, I suppose we all readily can. So, you think you're safe if you use a deodorant, but how can you be *sure*? Haven't we all "smelled that smell" at one time or another on some hapless "sure" soul? As one ad states, the chilling reality is: ***Others detect body odor*—the offender doesn't.**

But how could this happen? Don't we all know the basics of hygiene? How to handle a bar of soap? I can understand how this could happen after strenuous exercise or being trapped in a hot room while wearing a mohair sweater, but when it comes to the average day, ***should*** we have cause for concern?

…Care to hazard a guess? The answer, of course, is yes. It turns out that anybody can become the silent offender due to a simple lack of knowledge of biology. A 1949 advertisement alerted we, the ignorant public, with this terrifying message: Doctors find B.O. on 13 parts of the body! I can only imagine what people were thinking when their doctors informed them of this.

What! ***Thirteen???*** We're all doomed. Which thirteen? *Are* there thirteen parts of the body? The ad provides no further details. What could they be? I'll try to figure it out for all of us.

13 Smelly Places

1. **Arm Pits**
2. **Mouth**
3. **Nose (it smells smells, at least)**
4. **Private Region(s) (1 or 2?) (More?)**
5. **Feet**
6. **Scalp**
7. **Ears**

   (running out of ideas...)

8. **Belly Button (so I've heard)**
9. **Fingers**
10. **Knees**
11. **Elbows**

    (what's left?)

12. **Chest**
13. **Appendix**

This list is depressing. It takes me back to that fateful day in grade school when all the girls were herded into one assembly and the boys into another. We were shown a film that explained how something super special would soon be happening to us. We would blossom into women and be able to experience one of life's greatest gifts, the ability to have babies. However, the tradeoff would be brand-new body hair, wide hips, terrifying mood swings, painful periods with cramps, constipation, limited physical activities once a month (horseback riding is out) and — accompanying all this — all kinds of new body odor. Regular bathing was no longer optional (as many pre-pubescent kids liked to think) and it was time to invest in some deodorant. What a lot of responsibility! Well, we all have to grow up, but keeping track of thirteen places emitting body odor is overwhelming. Surely a potential mate would understand if a teeny whiff escaped from one's elbows, right? Aren't we all human?

At this point, I'm wondering if I should ever leave the house again. Social networking sounds better all the time. After all, even a glamorous-looking gal could be deemed "pathetic" due to her sloppy perspiration. A Swiss study revealed that men's B.O. smells like cheese whereas women's smells like onions. That makes for a classic combination atop a burger, but unfortunately, apparently even the slightest trace of armpit odor (always noticeable within three feet, I have read) will mar the most charming impression made from a distance and send a suitor reeling away in repulsion. How can you be sure you'll be ready when your soul mate arrives?

Due to this uncertainty, the public's desire to cloak themselves in fragrance has spawned a multi-billion-dollar industry. Fragrances are sold to make a woman more alluring, more confident, or just… different. The popularity of fragrances is the bane of people with allergies, but it seems most people would rather risk the wrath of those sensitive souls than risk not passing the 3-Foot Circle Test.

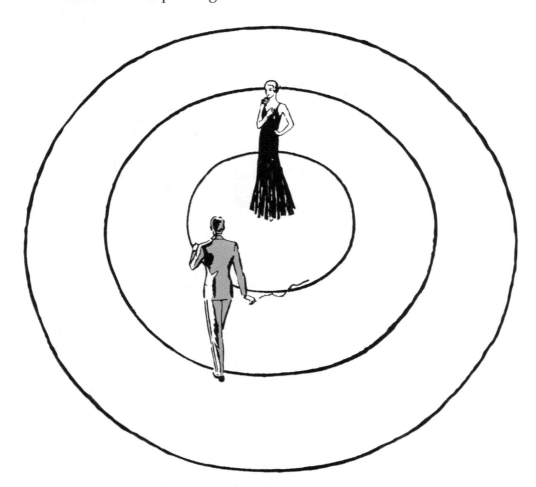

At 6 feet—LOVE AT FIRST SIGHT!
At 3 feet—ONE THING BREAKS THE SPELL

3-Foot Circle Test . . . Even a trace of armpit odor (always noticeable within three feet) will mar the most charming impression made from a distance. And the person who needs a deodorant can rarely sense that need herself.

The Heartbreak of Halitosis

To make matters worse, even the most beautiful doll can fall victim to bad breath, and just like B.O., it's hard for the offender to know she is perpetrating the crime. A woman with a momentary bout of halitosis who is getting the "hands off" treatment on an important date might go home cursing her inadequate bustline or Daddy's nose, never realizing it was that cup of coffee she sipped before she left the house. The safest strategy seems to be to eat nothing on a date, but what happens when you pass out on the dance floor? And can't an empty stomach also cause bad breath from the churning digestive acids? Even if you leave for the date fresh as spring, what happens if your date takes you to a great Thai restaurant and you're craving the Garlic Lovers Special? All you can do is propose that you both share it. One must be ever vigilant to win this war one battle at a time.

The Scent of a Woman

Sometimes it takes a furious man with pince-nez glasses to give us a wake-up call about our false sense of confidence. Ads say feminine hygiene is the foundation of both health *and* charm! Who knew? One thing I do know — it's going to take a lot more than a quick gargle and a dab of deodorant to pass muster when a suitor gets much, much closer than that three-foot circle.

So Few Women Understand
Yet Feminine Hygiene is the foundation of health and charm!
— **Science's Gift to Women** —

The term "feminine hygiene" was a euphemism for birth control back in the day before it could be discussed more frankly in ads. Douching with antiseptic fluids was thought to fight off those pesky sperm cells. So, it can be tricky from the modern perspective to entirely decode the advertisements. However, "feminine odor" was usually cited as a problem that could drive apart even the most loving marriages.

Just because no one has ever hinted that you have a feminine odor problem... doesn't necessarily mean that you might not have one.

Isn't the term "feminine odor" an oxymoron? How could we exquisitely feminine creatures have "feminine odor," as opposed to an enchanting "feminine scent," which is what the term originally meant? We rarely hear about "masculine odor" except in a rugged, endearing way. This is a female thing. Over the years, we have been told repeatedly that odor is at the root of relationship problems, and it's hard enough to make relationships work, right? There must be a way to hide this. And so, industries are born. Not only are there douches, there are sprays to help disguise that thunder from down under, feminine odor. And if you think anyone's going to clue you in about this odor when they won't even mention your breath or B.O., you are seriously delusional.

It's never too late for a wife to learn
these intimate physical facts!

Keep It Under Your Hat

SCALP ODOR—
Not you?

YOUR HAT HAS THE
inside story

It's so easy to have scalp odor—*and not know it!* But if you want the real truth as to whether *you* offend, just consult your hat.

Let's say your breath passes the romance test, but the object of your affections is still repulsed by you. What could it be *now?!?!* It could be S.O. **Scalp Odor.**

I see how this could be an issue back in the day. Gentle shampoo is a relatively modern convenience, so women used to soap their hair sparingly in order to retain their hair's luster. In the 1942 beauty book *Glorify Yourself* by Eleanore King, she discusses how frequently one should shampoo one's hair. She cites how some movie stars have their hair washed every day while other women with beautiful hair wash it once every six months with a twenty-brush cleaning twice a week. She recommends once every two weeks as a good general target. Hm… do you smell something? I sure do.

I remember my mom trying to preserve her salon hairstyles in the 1960s and 70s. Her hair was usually teased high in a bouffant style that seemed impossible to maintain at bedtime. She doused it in hairspray, secured it with a minefield of bobby pins, and wrapped it in toilet paper before her head hit the pillow. This is probably how she developed insomnia! She couldn't wash it at home without losing its style, so she only had it shampooed at the salon, which I recall was no more than every 2–3 weeks. If it toppled over during that period, she wore starchy wigs to cover it up, no matter the weather.

Although most women these days wash their hair more often than twice a year, scalp odor is still an issue, judging by my online research. I laughed at the title of a news story in my search results: "How to Tell if You Smell." News you need to know!

Foot Note*

Hey! What about smelly feet! Did you know that each of us have over two million sweat glands, and a whopping 250,000 of them are in our feet? This can only lead to F.O., **Foot Odor**, otherwise known as bromhidrosis. And F.O. leads directly to S.O. #2, **Shoe Odor**.

For such a famously odiferous zone, I have not found any advertisements or articles targeted at F.F.O., **Female Foot Odor**, nor any chipping away at women's self-esteem over this issue. Strange when you consider all the attention women give to every other type of odor. Maybe because some people are turned on by the smell of a woman's feet? But some people are also turned on by the smell of a man's feet. Is this the one issue that we as a society have agreed to not include in the Hall of Shame in which all other bodily failings reside?

Maybe this is because children are notorious for coming home with smelly shoes, socks, and feet. F.O. is not one of those odors that start with the onset of puberty. This odor is "all in the family" and one that contributes to the final topic on odor, the dreaded H.O., **House Odor**.

Stop Bad Foot Odor!

Ask Etta

Dear Mrs. Kitt ~ I have a lover who says sniffing my feet is a big turn on. Should I be worried?

*Sincerely,
Cinderella*

Dear Princess:
Sorry about stepping on your fairy tale fantasies, but if someone thinks your feet are the best-smelling part of your body, I shudder to think what the rest of you smells like! Buy yourself a bar of soap.

*

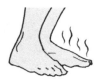

Don't Forget — Your Home Stinks Too

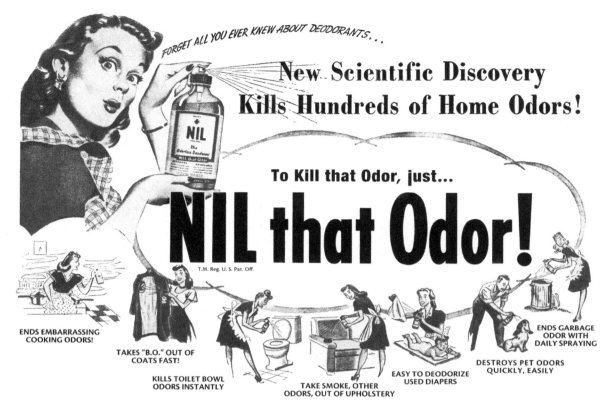

Yes, even when you are 100% fresh as a daisy from top to bottom and inside out, advertisers will always be there to remind you of this grim fact: the odors in your home *also* speak volumes about you. Yes, even those fumes coming out of your dog tell others just who you are. So be sure to spray everything! You, your clothes, your furniture, your garbage, your kitchen, your bathroom, your kids — *everything!*

Once you're done, give yourself a pat on the back for a job well done… then get up and start all over again! Personal hygiene is much like painting the Golden Gate Bridge. By the time you're done from end to end, it's time to start all over again. Feeling exhausted? Me too.

BATHROOM — No more embarrassing odors–thanks to GOOD-AIRE's amazing split-second action!

KITCHEN — Even cabbage, cauliflower, onions, fish odors vanish with one quick GOOD-AIRE spray.

Hello, Old Friend

Unsightly fat. It's been around a long time… a *very long time*. … And the bad news? It doesn't look like it's going anywhere anytime soon.

All my life I've heard this cry in advertisements: "Get rid of unsightly fat!" Always "unsightly fat" or similar. What exactly is "unsightly fat"? And how does it differ from "sightly fat"? Is there such a thing as "sightly fat"? I had to investigate.

First, I wondered who the genius was that coined the term, so I began searching the archives. The earliest mention I found was a news story from 1856 regarding an exhibition of the Yorkshire Agricultural Society. Reportedly, first prize went to a three-year-old ox that was a "wonderful animal of his age that did not exhibit the unsightly fat which was noticed in some of the other animals." I wonder if the other animals went on a crash diet after reading that story.

Nobody saw the value of exploiting this phrase until the early 1900s when the idea of unsightly fat on people began to take hold. Advertisers blamed it on a lack of muscle tone. Home remedies included a course of graceful walking. Exercise makes sense; however, the walking had to be *graceful*. Well, if this were true, then how did that three-year-old ox cut such a striking figure? What was its secret!

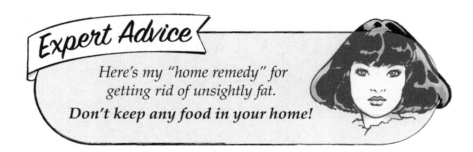

Expert Advice

Here's my "home remedy" for getting rid of unsightly fat.

Don't keep any food in your home!

In 1908, Druft's Reduction Pills upped the drama of unsightly fat by warning us that many people during the heated season suffered untold discomfort and sickness from it. In 1909, the Millard System of Beauty Culture lumped in the curse of unsightly fat with a slew of other flaws that could be eliminated by sending away to learn the secret of a European system unknown to the unsightly American woman. ***Why were we the last to know!***

Since that time, the ads for every unsightly fat remedy have assured women that it's easy to dispose of as long as you either:

1.) learn a certain secret that other women have been keeping from you
2.) follow a special reducing plan that a scientist or glamour girl has figured out, *or*
3.) take a modern pill that either keeps you from eating, or, better yet — lets you pig out while losing weight!

Good News for Fat Folks!
If You Want to Reduce Ten to Sixty Pounds Easily and Quickly, Read This

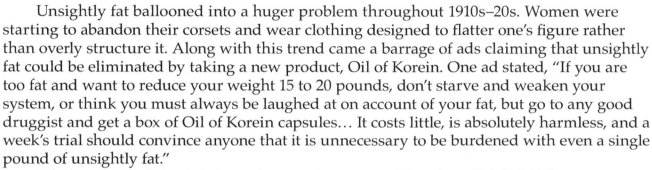

Unsightly fat ballooned into a huger problem throughout 1910s–20s. Women were starting to abandon their corsets and wear clothing designed to flatter one's figure rather than overly structure it. Along with this trend came a barrage of ads claiming that unsightly fat could be eliminated by taking a new product, Oil of Korein. One ad stated, "If you are too fat and want to reduce your weight 15 to 20 pounds, don't starve and weaken your system, or think you must always be laughed at on account of your fat, but go to any good druggist and get a box of Oil of Korein capsules… It costs little, is absolutely harmless, and a week's trial should convince anyone that it is unnecessary to be burdened with even a single pound of unsightly fat."

What was Oil of Korein? According to *Nostrums and Quackery, Vol. II* (1921), it came in red gelatin capsules containing a few drops of a mixture that was essentially 40 percent oil of sassafras (banned in the U.S. since 1960 for use in commercially mass-produced food and drugs as a potential carcinogen) and 60 percent liquid petrolatum (mineral oil). Despite the promises that the dieter need not diet, the directions that came with it recommended dietary restrictions, e.g. cutting starchy foods which "it is helpful to avoid." According to the American Medical Association, "Probably, in common with most obesity 'cures', any reduction that may follow the use of Oil of Korein is due to either the dieting or to impaired digestion."

By the 1920s, ridicule of overweight people was apparently at an all-time high because advertisements often mentioned that they were laughed at, called "fatty," and generally not considered in the same category as "normal people."

43

There's No Mystery About WHY You Are Fat!

Doctors tell us that in most cases you are fat because you eat too much EXTRA FATTENING HIGH-CALORIE FOODS. It's as simple as that!

Reach for Sweetreets Every Time You're Tempted to Eat or Drink Too Much!

"GET THEE BEHIND ME, SATAN!" How many times a day are you tempted to eat or drink? Too often, you must admit . . . and with disastrous results! You just can't resist! As a result, you get fatter and fatter with each extra bite!

As female society lumbered along through the 20th century, miracle cure after miracle cure continued to be discovered while we continued to be reminded that unsightly fat was all our fault. In this chapter I'll guide you through a mere sampling of the myriad of unsightly fat solutions that women have tried throughout the years.

MAKE THIS TEST NOW *With Your Own Hands!*

Interlock the fingers of both hands over abdomen, as in illustration, then press upwards and in gently, but firmly! Feel better? Of course you do! And that's what the new Slimtex Abdominal Supporter Belt does for you! Only Slimtex does it better! Send coupon today and test it at home!

Do You Look "Out of Shape"?

Do You Feel Droopy? Tired?

Try the Magic Help of Adjus-to-Slim

Get Rid of Surplus Fat! *Food Expert* Tells How

Who's to Blame? YOU!

**Can't Eliminate Surplus
Fat While Eating
Pastry**

By BEATRICE FAIRFAX

In 1924, columnist Beatrice Fairfax (the original Dear Abby) observed that women were overweight mainly because they ate too many chocolate shakes and pies for lunch without any thought of the consequences. Ms. Fairfax drew this conclusion by observing a sampling of American womanhood at a soda fountain one day while she ate a "sensible, but hasty lunch" (a long, cold glass of buttermilk and a Swiss cheese sandwich on rye). First, she watched a "shabby but distinguished-looking Englishwoman" who was "thin, trim, scrupulously neat and delightfully courteous to the boy behind the counter" eat a meager lunch of a ham sandwich and coffee. So far so good. She got Beatrice's seal of approval.

However, after this came the horror show of a "pasty-faced girl who had augmented her lack of beauty with peroxide on her hair, lilac powder to accent her pallor, blackened eyelashes and a general air of eagerness to look attractive." This brassy trollop "rushed in, banged on the counter with her vanity case to get the waiter's attention and then ordered in a gay, reckless, challenging voice which told that she was ready to make advances to any man — behind or in front of a soda fountain" and cried…

"The usual!"

And guess what "the usual" was? Let's all judge her together: a chocolate ice cream soda and a jelly doughnut. Yes, the "pasty complexion was accounted for."

Long editorial made short — this pasty low-class trollop wasn't the exception to the rule. Seven out of eleven women (yes — *63.636363636364 percent!*) plopped down and engorged themselves on chocolate sodas (yum) along with doughnuts and/or pie. One woman had the gall to do it even though she had *"three rolls of unsightly fat on the back of her neck!"* What the hell!

The moral of this article? Watch out for people taking notes when you eat out!

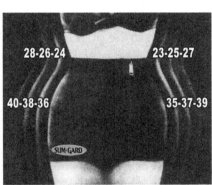

CONFESSIONS OF A FORMER FAT SLOB

Go ▷ Ask Etta

Dear Mrs. Kitt ~ I'm a girl with a healthy appetite, and I don't like "rabbit food." I've always heard that we need "good fat" in our diet. Is there anything wrong with that?

*Signed,
Curvy Girl*

Sorry, Curvy –
The only **"good fat"** is on your next-door neighbor!

Squeeze It, Steam It, Shake It!

Squeezing in unsightly fat dates back to 1600 BCE, as evidenced by a Cretan figurine of a Minoan snake goddess wearing a corset. So, it's no wonder that women's shapewear is a mainstay of fashion. The modern girdle was born at the start of the 20th century and rocketed in popularity for decades until Women's Liberation brought the love affair to a screeching halt. However, the girdle never entirely went away, and these days shapewear is the thing, with a variety of stretchy garments available to tuck you in and curve you out. Whatever impression you're after, there's shapewear to help create it.

Along the way, some products have promised to not only squeeze you in, but to reduce at the same time. In 1924, the Madame X girdle claimed to massage away unsightly fat while you wore it. ("Madame X" probably inspired by the sensual Madame X portrait by John Singer Sargent.) It claimed to make you **look thin while getting thin**. Hm. Really? Well, as they explain in the ad, "There is nothing else like it!" So there. As a bonus — an "interesting booklet" came free with your purchase.

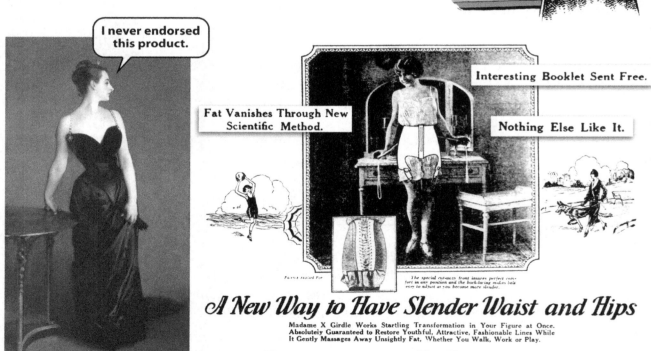

The same people who brought you the Mark Eden Bust Developer also brought you weight loss products such as Vacu-Pants, the Vib-A-Way tummy toner, and Sauna Belt Hot Pants. Another company sold a Swedish cream to reduce your measurements through self-massage. These old ads are the source of much amusement on social media, but products similar to these are still being sold. I can't tell you what works or doesn't work, but I can say that the battle against unsightly fat is one that rages on to this day. Nothing has changed.

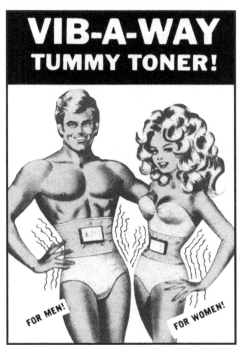

Have You Tried the Latest Diet?

The concept of dieting dates back to the 2nd century AD with Greek physician Soranus of Ephesus (*great name!*), who considered obesity a disease and prescribed laxatives, massage, and exercise to treat it. The world has changed so much since then, except for the desire to diet. While the desire has remained constant, the diets have constantly changed. Ask people which diet they recommend. Everyone has an opinion and an amazing success story to go with it. So, why do the diets keep changing? It seems that no diet is more exciting and more promising than the latest to come along.

Each new diet is always advertised as a scientific breakthrough that is more than a diet — it's a lifestyle. I've been on this planet long enough to assure you that it is not. Even if a diet works, people get bored and move on. That doesn't mean that all diets are bad or that it's foolish to watch one's weight, but some diets **are** bad and can lead to depression and more weight gain. So, many women are left endlessly chasing after the Great Diet Plan. Has this happened to you? Scan this list of diets and see how many you have tried. The number will most likely depend on your age. Are you thinking about trying one right now?

DIET SCORECARD
HOW MANY HAVE YOU TRIED?

❑ Stillman	❑ Beach Body	❑ DASH	❑ Spirulina
❑ Paleo	❑ Grapefruit	❑ Raw Food	❑ Morning Banana
❑ Pritikin	❑ 4-Hour Body	❑ Nutrisystem	❑ Nordic
❑ Keto	❑ Whole30	❑ Cabbage Soup	❑ Scarsdale
❑ South Beach	❑ Cambridge	❑ Martha's Vineyard	❑ 5:2
❑ Atkins	❑ Mediterranean	❑ Salisbury	❑ Alkaline
❑ Zone	❑ Weight Watchers	❑ Ayd's Diet Candy	❑ Apple Cider Vinegar
❑ Superfood	❑ Juice Cleanse	❑ Slim-Fast	❑ Blood Type
❑ Macrobiotic	❑ Drinking Man's	❑ Master Cleanser	❑ Cigarette
❑ Dukan	❑ Jenny Craig	❑ Detox	❑ Sleeping Beauty
❑ Sugar Busters	❑ Volumetrics	❑ Flexitarian	❑ Baby Food

Featured on T.V., Radio, Magazines - Doctor's astonishing diet discovery !!!

Q Is it a fad, or can I get real and lasting results on the Cambridge Diet?

The Pritikin regimen for a long, healthy life

YOU CAN'T HIDE FAT CLUMSY ANKLES

When tempted to over-indulge
"Reach for a Lucky instead"

Be moderate—be moderate in all things, even smoking. Avoid that future shadow by avoiding over-indulgence, if you would maintain that modern, ever-youthful figure. "Reach for a Lucky instead."

Lucky Strike, the finest Cigarette you ever smoked, made of the finest tobacco—The Cream of the Crop—"IT'S TOASTED." Lucky Strike has an extra, secret heating process. Everyone knows that heat purifies and so 20,679 physicians say that Luckies are less irritating to your throat.

"Coming events cast their shadows before"

LUCKY STRIKE "IT'S TOASTED" CIGARETTES

How'd you like to give those extra holiday pounds a nice HAWAIIAN PUNCH.? (LOW-CALORIE)

It wouldn't hurt. Especially after all that celebrating and overstuffing. LOW-CALORIE HAWAIIAN PUNCH is a satisfying fruit juicy liquid snack every bit as great as regular Hawaiian Punch. Don't you feel better already?

HAWAIIAN PUNCH LOW CALORIE

"IS THIS THE ANSWER?"
The Amazing Vitamin B-Kelp. Lecithin and Apple Cider Vinegar Diet.

(Advertisment)

LOSE UNSIGHTLY FAT AIR FORCE DIET
Often Called The Drinking Man's Diet

Make This Home Recipe To Take off Ugly Fat

FOR COMPULSIVE EATERS
THE ALL "NEW" for '72 IMPROVED

GRAPEFRUIT DIET

LOSE up to 10 LBS. IN 10 DAYS ONLY /$1.00

FOR LARGE APPETITES AND SMALL WAISTLINES

TaB

Suzanne Somers' EAT, CHEAT, AND MELT THE FAT AWAY

Avoid the Dangers of Bad Carbohydrates
Balance Your Hormone and Insulin Levels

ENTER THE ZONE

ROAD MAP TO

P.H.D.

LOW-CALORIE DESSERTS... SALADS... MAIN DISHES IN MODERN KNOX GEL-COOKERY

Silhouette Recipes

10 DAYS FREE TRIAL

NEW!

AYDS APPETITE SUPPRESSANT CANDY

natural chocolate flavor

NET WT 24 OZ (1½ LBS)/680 G

AYDS

Science Can't Fix Ugly Fat... Or Can It...?

The tempting alternative to dieting is to reduce while eating all the food you want. Since the 1930s, weight loss pills have been advertised as the way to get the figure of your dreams without the nuisance of exercise and the chore of modifying one's diet.

Taking a magic pill seems like a dream come true brought to you by Science. The diet pills of the 20th century typically were amphetamines, which came with risky side effects. The pills were marketed to appeal to the times, like the 1960s diet pill X-11 that sounded like something a spy would take to shrink to the size of a paper clip.

The ads also were tailored to the tastes of the times. In 1973, the weight loss remedy 1-2-3 screamed at women to "take that ugly FAT OFF" while feasting on "sensible food" such as veal scallopini and franks.

Yes! Meal planning solved.

If even the mere act of being conscious was too heavy a lift for you while dieting, some pills even promised that you could lose weight in your sleep! Life just gets better all the time.

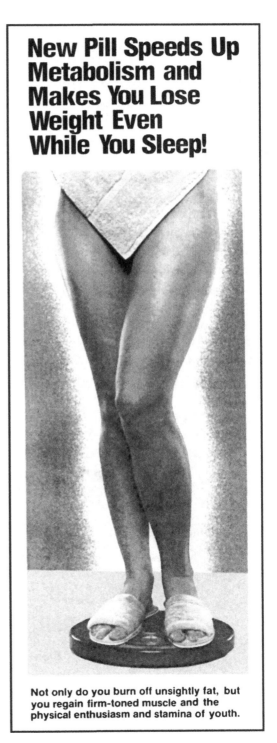

Feasting on veal scallopini might appeal to some diet-bound ladies, but what about those with a sweet tooth?

Ayds diet candy solved that problem. These chewy sweets were first sold in the 1930s as an appetite-suppressant candy. The suppressant was Benzocaine, which numbed one's taste buds. Over the decades glamorous Hollywood stars and glitterati promoted it. As improbable as it sounds, it was popular enough to still be sold in the grocery stores when I was a kid. I always wondered if the candy tasted good. I never found out. Ayds went out of business in the 1980s due to the outbreak of the AIDS epidemic. People couldn't get past the name, even when the name was changed to Diet Ayds. By this time, too, products such as SlimFast's diet shake were gaining in popularity. SlimFast wasn't the first diet shake — Sego was a popular liquid diet food of the 1960s that came with the slogan "Good for your ego." It may

The Fat Dress.

Yards and yards of loose, flowing material can cover up yards and yards of loose, flowing body. But like all cover-ups, it is only that. Underneath it all, you're fat. And it makes you feel bad. And you'd like to do something about it. Heaven only knows you've tried before. This diet. And that diet. Maybe even pills that promised to melt your extra pounds away. And nothing worked. Take heart. There is something that works.

Not a miracle. Not a drug.

It's the Ayds Plan. Not a magic wand. And not a drug. Simply a sensible, effective *Plan* to help you take fat off, and keep it off.

From 210 lbs... ...to 125 lbs.

First, there's the calorie-reduced diet. Then there's Ayds. A delicious, vitamin-enriched candy. One or two with a hot drink before meals stimulate the blood sugar apparatus in your body. And because Ayds helps take the edge off your appetite, you can eat less and take in fewer calories. And no matter what you've read or heard, that's the only sensible way to lose weight.

This plan has worked for literally thousands of women. The photos above of Cheryl Bruhn are just one example of what the Ayds Plan can do.

Why not put away that fat dress once and for all by putting Ayds® Reducing Plan Candy to work for you. Oh, you'll still have to work at it too. But at least you'll have help. Which might be just what it takes for you to win. And most of all, we want you to win.

We want you to win.

have been good for the ego, but bad for keeping dieters satisfied. It fell out of favor as dieters eventually lost their ability to subsist on Sego, a product not associated with delicious flavor.

SEGO
DIET DRINK

"VERY" Flavors
10-oz.

4 for $1

These days, the new diets just keep on coming. Weight loss plans feel like mastering chess. Theories abound on what to eat, when to eat it, when not to eat, and what to do while we are either eating or not eating. Some swear by "grazing," others by fasting. Some advocate liquid diets while others tout the importance of chewing. Will we ever find the answer? Imagine if this much thought and strategy were applied to world peace as they have been to vanquishing the eternal scourge, unsightly fat.

Unsightly Fat Sucks

A solution for those with unsightly fat deposits

"[Suction lipectomy] . . . is not a weight-reduction technique. It is only used to resilhouette the body."

Another popular modern method is to surgically suck out fat through liposuction. If you have the money and the ability to get it done, you can wave goodbye to your fat in just a few hours. Effective, but more expensive than a diet shake. How to persuade women to try it? Pull out the phrase that has persuaded women to try anything for over 100 years: *Unsightly fat!*

But at what cost to the planet? One can only hope that there is no illegal dumping of unsightly fat, as reported upon in 1995. One man's medical waste is another man's leftovers from a hamburger stand? I wonder who the lucky forensic scientist was who had to unravel the truth to this unsightly crime.

Another timeless way to motivate us to do something about our figures has been to remind us that even the perfect figure needs work… sooner or later. The sands of time are working against us even if we continue honing our bodies through healthy living each day. Can't we ever enjoy what we have now without someone out there reminding us that tomorrow is a few hours away? The answer is "no."

Unsightly fat in trash

RIVERSIDE, Calif. — There's no law against losing unsightly fat, but prosecutors took offense when someone left two pounds of it in a restaurant trash bin.

A hospital employee was charged Monday with illegally disposing of medical waste. Prosecutors said the waste included human fat scraps from liposuction surgery.

Prosecutors allege he tossed the water in the trash behind a Palm Desert hamburger restaurant on June 20.

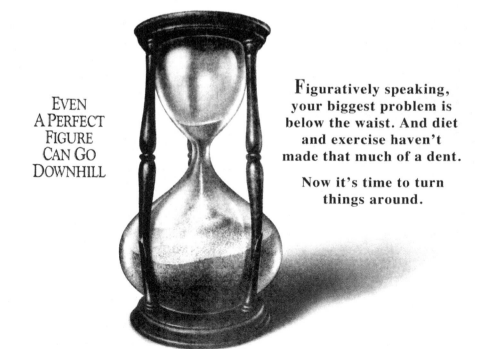

EVEN
A PERFECT
FIGURE
CAN GO
DOWNHILL

Figuratively speaking, your biggest problem is below the waist. And diet and exercise haven't made that much of a dent.

Now it's time to turn things around.

When All Else Fails... Exercise

A common theme with weight loss products is that the dieter can avoid what appears to be the worst thing imaginable — exercise. However, exercises to improve one's figure are another longstanding tradition.

In 1921, silent movie actress Doris Doscher (whose beauty claim to fame was to have posed as the goddess of Liberty on the United States quarter) offered this exercise to reduce the accumulation of fat under the arms: briskly rub away the fat while crossing your arms around the shoulders. If only it were that easy.

Slapping away fat was popularized in the 1920s by fitness coach to the stars, Sylvia of Hollywood. She claimed that squeezing and slapping away fat was the missing ingredient in weight loss regimens, and beauty guides from the time followed her lead by telling women to make sure they slapped while working out so that they eliminated that fat gained from all those doughnuts wolfed down at the lunch counter.

In 1968, beauty expert Josephine Lowman forecast the concept of aerobic dance when she advised women who "can't discipline themselves to do specific figure exercises" to exercise to music, even if they make up their own "silly movements," because "exercise isn't so much like work when done to a contagious beat." She added, "Just don't get so enthusiastic that you knock yourself out." Solid advice!

Fitness icon Jack LaLanne inspired a fitness revolution for housewives starting in the 1950s and 1960s with his daytime TV show. He advocated healthy eating along with exercises that women could do at home since the idea of women working out in public was considered by many at that time to be a shameful spectacle.

In 1964, a chiropractor named Richard Proctor launched the Elaine Powers Figure Salon chain, a women-only gym that focused on getting women down to their "correct dress size." Elaine Powers didn't exist, but the idea of her inspired women to get to the gym primarily to lose weight.

The fitness craze of the 1970s got women to start jogging, aerobic dancing, and weight training. The emphasis was now on fitness from the inside out and less about dress sizes. The 1980s was a decade of women's fitness as embodied by workout icon Jane Fonda. Home workouts on VHS tapes such as Buns of Steel sprang up. In the 1990s, home workouts gained more traction, with Pilates and new products such as Suzanne Somers' ThighMaster and the Bowflex home gym. Martial arts workouts grew in popularity, especially with Tae Bo. By the 2000s, gentler workouts in the form of yoga and barre took hold while military-style boot camp workouts also proliferated. With each year came new trends… spinning, CrossFit, Zumba… and more recently fitness trackers such as Fitbit. Anything goes these days, but much like diets, the public is most eager to embrace whatever is new in the pursuit of physical perfection.

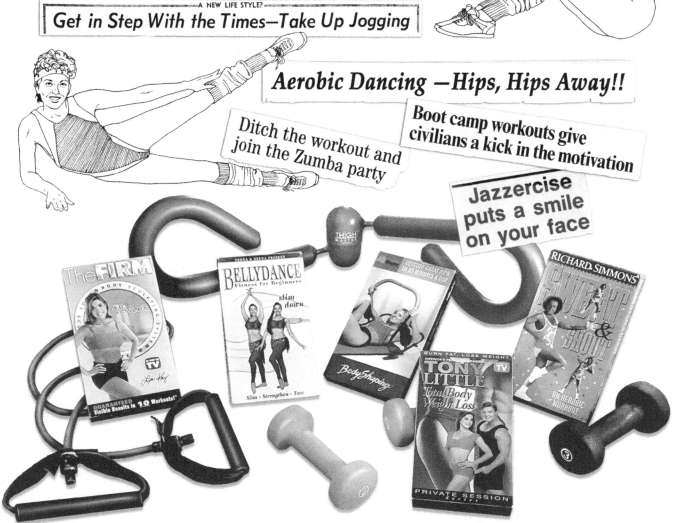

A NEW LIFE STYLE?

Get in Step With the Times—Take Up Jogging

Aerobic Dancing —Hips, Hips Away!!

Ditch the workout and join the Zumba party

Boot camp workouts give civilians a kick in the motivation

Jazzercise puts a smile on your face

55

The Secret to Happiness?

HEY! YOU SKINNY, PALE SICKLY FOLKS!

Hey, SKINNY!
Easy Way Puts On
Pounds and Inches Fast

So… with all these amazing diet and exercise programs at our disposal, how could we possibly go wrong? Well, guess what? Achieving and keeping the perfect figure requires walking a very fine line: Don't let them call you "Skinny"!

Eureka! We have finally found that there is indeed "sightly fat." The secret to happiness? It appears to be finding that happy medium. Who knows exactly what that is, though? It seems as if we are doomed to check the scale and fish for compliments to see if we've hit the mark. As usual, we just can't win.

In all seriousness, it does seem as if we're making some progress as a society in terms of appreciating all body types. We see curvy models and mannequins. Gyms and diets have been more focused on health rather than getting us into the "correct" dress size. Whether you want to gain, lose, or maintain your weight, it's all good as long as you're happy with the person you are. There are enough shamers out there without shaming yourself!

THE MEN RAN AWAY FROM HER SKINNY SHAPE!

DON'T BE FAT

6 WEEKS AGO
H-E-Y SKINNY
PEOPLE LAUGHED AT HER FIGURE AND SHE NEVER HAD A "DATE"

TODAY
NOW SHE HAS PLENTY OF FRIENDS AND SHE'S NOT ASHAMED TO BE SEEN

DON'T BE SKINNY

If you are skinny, thin and underweight because of poor eating habits, take New Wate-On. It's rich in weight gaining calories, vitamins, minerals, iron, quick energy elements and other weight building nutrients. Fast weight gains of 5-10-15 pounds and more reported, without pads, exercise or fishy tasting oils. And, as weight is added to cheeks, bust-line, arms, legs, hips, thighs and all the body, you should look better without that thin, skinny appearance. Satisfaction from first trial or return to store for refund.

Wanted Hair

Whatever it is, it's not what you have. Why is that? Shouldn't it make sense that the color and type of hair you were born with is the best frame for you? Yet so many of us spend thousands of dollars in our lifetime on changing the appearance of our hair. Go to any hair salon, and unless you are stubbornly resistant to change, chances are you will be walking out with a new style, possibly a new color, and a bag of expensive new hair products to make your look last longer than five minutes after you leave the building.

Boredom contributes to some of it. Fashion contributes to a lot of it. Sometimes thick, luxurious locks are in. Sometimes hair as flat as if it were ironed (and sometimes it has been) is in. Celebrities of the moment sometimes inspire a craze. Over the decades, popular styles have come and gone, eventually to come back again. Mary Pickford's long ringlets, Josephine Baker's bob, Jean Harlow's platinum blonde, Veronica Lake's peek-a-boo locks, Audrey Hepburn's pixie cut, Jackie Kennedy's bouffant, Farrah Fawcett's mane, Olivia Newton-John's perm, Jennifer Aniston's "Rachel," Pink's faux-hawk, Rhianna's pineapple ponytail… these are just a few of the styles that have sent women running to the salon.

Unfortunately, it's probable that you would look good in only one or two of these. What's a woman to do? Stick with what works and eventually become the old woman in the market sporting a blue bouffant? Or change with the times and risk complete humiliation? The dilemma never ends. No wonder so many women "hate their hair." It's an eternal work in progress.

Can You Ever Have Enough Hair?

Throughout my research, I have seen a recurring theme: the longing for longer hair… even longer, *longer* hair. Which strikes me as interesting because every stylist I have ever gone to has had an insatiable desire to cut my hair *shorter*. Based on my friends' hairdresser experiences, this seems to be universal. Hairdressers insist that shorter hair frames the face better, is healthier, moves more naturally, doesn't hang down, weighing down one's appearance, and is classier, cuter, and more in style. Then why do most of us sit there with a worried expression, warily asking, "How *much* do you want to cut off?" It can get tense. You really want to get along with your hairdresser and have things end well by the time you leave. You are the one with the money and the choice whether to ever return, but he or she is the one holding the scissors. I wonder how many of these ads got responses from women who wound up on the bad end of this power struggle. To be fair, damaged or chopped hair usually comes from home treatments. Home perms, home color, and home cuts are trouble waiting to happen. No matter what we do, we take a gamble whenever we mess with our tresses.

The Color of Boring

Hair color can be a big source of insecurity. Ninety percent of the population's hair color is black or brown, so it's no wonder advertisers prompt women to change to something lighter with campaigns such as "Is it true… blondes have more fun?" and "Some lucky girls are born red. Others catch up." Movies and sitcoms have often relied on the old plot device of the mix-up caused when a husband doesn't realize that the ravishing creature he's flirting with is his wife who wanted to surprise him with a new hair color. How many of us have wondered if our lives would be better if we changed the hue of our humdrum hair? Would this single act open doors that we never even knew existed?

Stereotypes based on hair color abound with vexing mixed messages. They call blondes dumb, but they are also considered very sexy. Redheads can be bullied as children, but they are considered fiery and sexy as women. Brunettes are associated with being smart, but they are boring and not as sexy as blondes and redheads.

In the 1920s, Anita Loos wrote the popular novel *Gentlemen Prefer Blondes*, followed by *But Gentlemen Marry Brunettes*. This concept has lingered throughout my lifetime. Blondes are sexier, but more fitting for a fling, than the sensible, practical brunette. However, I have found no reliable surveys of men that confirm this. I think this is mostly something in women's heads. I have been both colors. Going blonde did not dramatically change my life, so, as a natural brunette, I did the sensible thing — stopped spending my money on bleaching my hair.

These days, you can also dye your hair non-traditional colors like pink, blue, and purple, which instantly informs people, "I'm not boring." Which takes us back to the predicament: what chance does a poor ordinary brunette stand in the love arena?

Surveys have shown that most American women dye their hair, and hair color affects their self-confidence. How much of this is a dream and how much of this is real? Could hair color be the driving force behind a breakup? Must we keep up on this every minute of our lives? According to advertising, the answer is *yes!*

Are you the same blonde he had dinner with last week?
(…or has your shampoo faded the shade?)

The Autumn of Our Years

FORGOTTEN
(BECAUSE OF GRAY HAIR)

Clairol swiftly, surely secretly eliminates the heartaches of gray or graying hair.

Gray hair. The final frontier. What to do… *what to do!* The decision to go gray or run for cover is a divisive one with no right or wrong answer. We sprout gray at different times, sometimes as early as adolescence. You either like what's happening, or you don't, and your decision to cover the gray or go natural can be positively and negatively judged by others. You have no control over their reaction. Great. Just when you have developed a sense of personal style and confidence in how you wear your hair… *oops!* Here comes the gray. A new set of issues!

One of the most repeated messages to women for over 100 years is that the appearance of gray hair signals the **end**. The end of romance. The end of a career. The end of compliments. As one hair color ad from 1925 put it:

No wide-awake, life-loving woman wants to be classed as an 'old lady' . . . be crowded out by younger women . . . relegated to the shelf.

A chilling prospect indeed. Thanks for letting us know, hair color ads. However, there is a solution — spend money to cover the gray, and we can carry on. Bring on the hot sex!

The promotion and the raise! The people who think your daughter is your mother! Hooray for hair color! Well, I do think it's great that we have options. Let us have the choice. But as we cover the gray, there's always the worry that those roots are showing. Or that our neck and our hands will still give us away. Are we fooling anybody?

Many women spend their entire lives coloring their hair, first for fashion and later to cover the gray. Looking for a company to invest in? Consider one that sells hair color!

GO ▷ Ask Etta

Dear Mrs. Kitt ~ All my life I have been complimented on my chestnut hair. However, I feel like I'm in a rut. I want to go blonde. Some friends say I should do it. Others say it would be a mistake. I have tried on blonde wigs and think they look good. Should I go for it?

Sincerely,
Bored Brown

Dear Bored:
You're bored? How do you think I feel! Can't you think for yourself? I'm an advice columnist, not a psychic. Don't you have a mirror? Bleach it blonde, walk into a room, and see if anyone runs out screaming. You will have your answer.

Dry, Drab, Limp, Wilted, Curly, Frizzy, Thin, Thick… Help, I'm Feeling Sick!

do you sleep your sets away?

Whatever our color or style may be, all around us are reminders that our hair is "too" this and "not enough" that. Women with straight hair want it curly. Women with curly hair want it straight.

You might be absolutely gorgeous, but still have hair envy. I grew up hearing about how curly hair was considered the most beautiful. I have read surveys, I have heard love songs, and I have seen social experiments that reveal how people respond more favorably to a woman with curls than one with straight hair. Well, I have straight hair. Of course, this can be remedied. For all us straight-haired "Plain Janes," stores are overflowing with products that curl one's hair and hold it. When I was young, I put up my hair in rollers and baked it under the bonnet of our home hair dryer every night. Sometimes I braided it to give it waves. Later, I set it with hot rollers. After that, I got a disastrous perm that scorched off about one-third of my hair. The rest never grew back.

When I was in college I had a friend with naturally thick wavy hair. To my surprise, she had spent her youth punishing her hair with chemical relaxers and irons because she had hair envy for straight hair! Why do we spend all this

time, money, and hassle chasing after whatever it is we don't have? It's not that one type of hair is better; it's that we hate our hair. When I do an online search for "hate your hair" I get 1,120,000 results! What did our poor "crowning glory" do to deserve this?

As we curl and straighten our hair year after year, the inevitable happens and we damage it. Now we have **that** to contend with. Frizzies! Split ends! Dull lifeless hair! We then engage in hair care rituals and buy more products to fix all this. No wonder many women leave their home in a funk or never leave at all because they are having a "bad hair day."

What goes up must come down, and so it goes with our hair as we run back and forth to the store to create our fantasy hairstyle, hold the darned thing in place, then repair whatever damage we created in the process. How many hours in our lives have been spent struggling to make hair longer, shorter, bigger, flatter, smoother, fluffier, or just plain *completely different!*

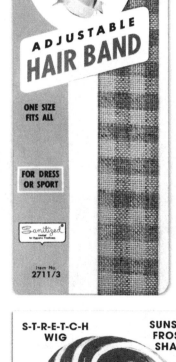

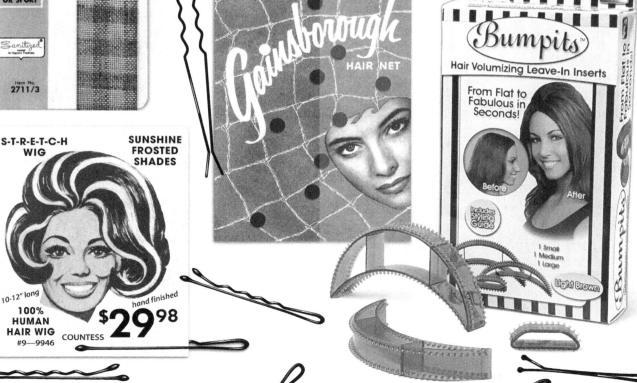

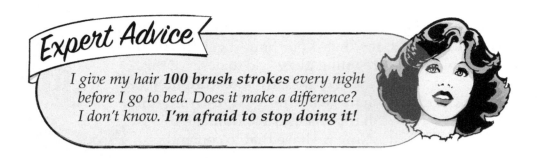

How to Get Wanted Hair? It's Easy!

I conclude this part of the chapter with a handy list of tips that I have gleaned for obtaining thick, long, shiny hair. By the time you're done, your hair will be tasty enough to eat!

massage scalp • shampoo with egg • sleep on silk pillows • eat lots of protein • wrap wet hair in a T-shirt • deep condition hair once a week • avoid hot styling tools • rinse hair with lemon juice • use a hair mask before working out • moisturize hair with avocado • no rubbing • shampoo with baking soda • use a boar bristle brush • detangle with your fingers • don't wash hair every day • UV protect your hair • use a leave-in conditioner • brush hair twice a day • eat lots of salmon • rinse hair with vinegar • take hair vitamins • moisturize hair with bananas • only shampoo the scalp • trim hair every six to eight weeks • wash hair with lukewarm water • moisturize hair with coconut oil • no blotting • don't put conditioner near the roots • rinse hair thoroughly after washing • moisturize hair with mayonnaise • change your part from time to time • exfoliate your scalp • use a hair mask • no pulling • rinse hair with beer • reduce stress • • • *buy a wig!*

Unwanted Hair — The Root of All Evil

The world of hair breaks down into two basic categories: wanted hair and unwanted hair. Could there be anything on our bodies that is fickler than hair? We have roughly five million hair follicles from head to toe, and out of those five million, how many are a big disappointment, a total embarrassment, and/or a continual nuisance? Hair on the head may have its own share of problems, but hair everywhere else almost always falls into the realm of *"get rid of it!"*

If it seems as though modern society puts too much emphasis on hair removal, you should know that in ancient Egypt a hairless head and body was considered the ideal in beauty. These women, most famously Cleopatra, used a variety of techniques including shaving and body sugaring to be completely smooth and bald. *51 BC problems!*

Hair removal on various parts of the body remained a mainstay of fashion throughout the centuries, but modern standards of women's shaving in the U.S. kicked into gear at the start of the 20th century with the introduction of shorter hemlines and sleeveless dresses. The need to shave became official in 1914 when Gillette introduced the Milady Décolleté, the first razor for women, and informed them that smooth underarms were now one of the "necessities" of perfect grooming. Not only did women need smooth underarms, they also had to worry about hairy forearms. *Nooooo!* Didn't we have enough to worry about already?

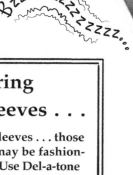

300,000 **hair follicles down . . . only 3 million more to go!**

Bzzzzzzzzzzzzzzzz...

Up, Up, and Away!

In many ways, the 20th century was an exciting time for women's progress, with more opportunities in careers and more freedom to dress (or undress) as they pleased. Take, for example, women's bathing suits, which shrank decade by decade as if they had been accidentally tossed in the dryer.

THE String bikini

In the 1900s, women were going to the beach in a bathing dress, bloomers and stockings. No need to shave! As the decades progressed, women abandoned this and wore tank-styled suits with shorts covering the thighs. In the pre-World War II years, they began wearing two-piece suits as seen in pinups. In 1946, the French bikini made its debut. After that, suits continued to get skimpier, with the itsy bitsy teenie weenie yellow polka dot bikini of the 60s, the string bikini of the 70s, and the thong of the 80s and beyond.

As more and more skin became exposed, more and more hair needed to be removed. But how? It isn't all that difficult to remove hair. The tricky issue is how to remain silky smooth at all times. The "wanted" hair follicles on your head range from 90,000–150,000. That leaves over **four million** unwanted follicles to reckon with.

The dream of permanently removing unwanted hair was realized when electrolysis was invented in 1875. Considering this, why doesn't every woman who has some unwanted hair get this procedure? Part of the answer goes to time and cost. Another part of the answer is — *ow!!!* If only there were a way to pull out hair or kill hair that didn't involve some level of pain. Women have their own preferences for what they are willing to tolerate. Some shave, some wax, some use depilatories, some use lasers and light therapies, and on it goes. The amount of time, money, and pain spent on hair removal is enough to make your hair curl.

Bare Down There

> **Like it? Wait 'til you see what I did *up higher!***

As time marched on, and we continued step-by-step to return to the beauty ideals of the ancient Egyptians, I suppose the trend to shave *everything* was inevitable. It came with the introduction of the Brazilian wax in 1987 when the J. Sisters salon opened in New York City and taking it all off took off.

I have read that the popularity of porn over the years also led to the trend to go bald "down under." With this, women now have to contend with yet another way to be judged due to their hair choices. The worst thing about this is that you can't tell what the latest trend is without either reading up on it or asking people. The latter is a topic of conversation I imagine would be reserved for close friends, but what do your friends know, really? Let's say you're dating and sexually active. How can you know whether your first-time partner will appreciate what you've done or not done? You might not get kicked out of bed, but will you get called back for a second date?

Life keeps getting more complicated. What to do? Let nature "run wild"? Go bare, if you dare? Or delve into the art of creative ladyscaping? Do you shave it into a playful design like a lightning bolt, martini glass, heart, mohawk, postage stamp, Bermuda Triangle, or landing strip? The risk you take is when you shed your clothes and what you thought was a trendy style is laughed at as "so yesterday." Perhaps it's best to come up with your own designs? I have a few ideas.

Ladyscaping Ideas

Hair, There, and Everywhere

Before closing, I must address the frustrating world of facial hair. Some women battle unwanted moustaches and beards for most of their lives, but even if one's face is peachy smooth in one's youth, weird things may start to happen as the years pass by. Long wiry hairs sprout in the eyebrows, and hairs start popping out of the chin in a "mad scientist" sort of way. Just when you think you've shaved and plucked them all, you check your face later in the mirror in the bright light outside and find Abe Lincoln staring back at you.

Many women prefer bleaching to removing facial hair, but many also use a wide range of home and salon strategies to remove it.

Some women embrace their facial hair, but many consider it a source of embarrassment. What is it about a single hair where it shouldn't be that sends us running to the bathroom when we also spend hours making all the rest of our hair as eye-catching as possible? It's like finding a hair in your meal. The only wanted hair is where you want it to be!

Which reminds me —

Where's my hair spray?

HORRIFYING QUOTE ABOUT HAIR #3

A woman might have a man's brain and hold a man's position in the business world, but let one little hair appear on her face, she will go through untold agony to be rid of it.

~1914 beauty column

ZAP! ZAP! ZAP! ZAP!

What Men Want

What *do* men want when it comes to a wife? A true-blue heart? A great cook? Huge hooters? Luscious lips? Sure, these things can lead to a second date, but what sets a woman apart from "date bait" and "wedded bliss"?

Through the course of my research I unlocked the secret. Lovely hands. Soft and creamy, with beautiful nails and no freckles, spots, or wrinkles. Men are irresistibly drawn to them.

I know this is hard to believe, but after poring through scads of vintage ads, I have learned that there are hands — and then there are *honeymoon* hands. Wishing for a wedding ring? Make sure you have hands that are pretty enough for one.

As with all beauty goals, maintaining lovely hands requires constant work. It gets even more difficult after one's wedding day. Now a woman must deal with the challenge of battling dishpan hands, an issue made even more difficult for the "2-Job" women of the Great Depression who had to ensure that their hands looked flawless at their secretarial job during the day while toiling through the drudgery of housework at night. Modern day women also have to contend with this — will we be judged negatively if our hands are chapped, even if it were due to a good cause? Could we stamp "EXEMPT" on our nails to excuse us after rescuing puppies in a muddy storm?

IN VENICE... a Hand Kiss... and

I felt like a movie star! On the Piazza San Marco, an Italian I'd met came up and kissed my hand. Jim (this American boy) said, *"Pretty silly, this handkissing."* But later—

Jim took both my hands. *"M-m—soft,"* he said. *"Maybe nice to kiss such soft hands."* It shows—I was smart to use Jergens Lotion and keep my hands nice. Because—

One dreamy night in a gondola Jim said he really loves me. *"Never let any other man kiss your darling hands,"* he said. *"They're mine now."* And

What Do Your Hands Say about You?

Consider the plight of the hardworking career woman of the past… the one often portrayed in movies who was hoping someday her boss would notice her. Smart, stylish, hardworking, loyal, and down-to-earth. Why, oh why, did her boss not notice her? If only I could reach through the movie screen and tell her: *moisturize your hands!*

> I would marry you, Miss Jones — but *those chapped hands!*

How important are lovely hands to women? A report from 2015 revealed that women spent over **seven million dollars a year** on nail polish! Considering there is a nail salon on almost every corner, it's safe to say lovely hands are pretty darn important. Surveys show that most men don't really pay much attention to women's nails, but some employers may judge you based on the grooming of your hands.

A manicure does say a lot about you. Some women stay neutral with the French manicure and pale colors. Then there are those who show they're nonconformists with a wave of the hand. Could your hands make the difference between success or failure in romance and career? Does one's fate hang on a hangnail? Again, advertisers say *yes!*

The Tell-tale Hands

Even if your nails are sending the right message, what are your hands saying? According to the 1965 column "The Feminine Look," you really have to watch what your hands are doing:

Your Hands on Display

What impression do your hands make? Do you realize that next to your face, your hands are the most expressive characteristic? […] It takes practice to acquire the art of knowing how to use your hands gracefully. Are your hands attractive and graceful when you are seated, standing, walking, or shaking hands?

Graceful Hands Accent Natural Attractiveness

This same message is echoed through beauty books and columns of the past. They even provide exercises to develop your hands' graceful charm. *Yay! Another set of exercises to do each day!*

But even if your hands are as graceful as the wings on birds, this can't stop them from revealing your age. So, as women grow older, they become concerned with the appearance of age spots, wrinkles, and veins on those "hands on display." All our lives we are told to hide or fix signs of that dirty little secret, aging. My grandmother always said a lady never reveals her age, and she made sure of it by wearing gloves when she went out.

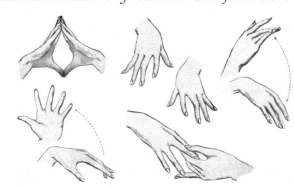

Exercises to Develop Graceful Hands

Those Horrid Age Spots
"I was so embarrassed, I served lunch with my gloves on."

DO YOUR HANDS REVEAL YOUR AGE?

Hands Can Reveal Your Age

Be your age, but don't look it, if you are over thirty! Do you see signs of vanishing youth...

For Aging Hands

The Right to Bare Arms

Exercising flabby arms

With all the focus on hands, you would think that people aren't scrutinizing the appendages that lead to them. But *au contraire*, the arms are another focal point for low self-esteem. Call them bat wings, sails, or bingo wings — flabby arms are yet another issue we are told we must combat. If we fail, we are advised to wear loose, long-sleeved attire like a shroud to hide them from view. The message we receive is that people will think less of us if they glimpse a jiggle as we reach for an appetizer at our nephew's wedding.

The classic cure for bat wings is exercise, but women also tighten and tone with fillers, firming creams, arm lift surgery, ultrasound, and radiofrequency (RF) treatments. The time period of 2000–2012 saw a dramatic upswing in women getting arm lift procedures (*over 4,000 percent!*) due to First Lady Michelle Obama's well-toned arms. It was suddenly "in" to have them thin and trim.

If you don't have the money or interest in these procedures, then it's time to grab some dumbbells, hop on a weight machine, or learn circus tricks to add tone to those troubled upper arms.

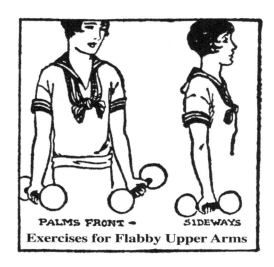

PALMS FRONT → SIDEWAYS
Exercises for Flabby Upper Arms

Do This a Few Times Daily and Flabby Arms Will Disappear.

You Don't Have a Leg to Stand On

Legs are another feature of the female anatomy often sung about, talked about, and touted as a key to devastating female appeal. These legs of legend are always long and lean, which is fine and dandy if you possess them, but what do you do if you don't? Advertisers, gyms, and beauty experts insist we can have any figure we desire if we exert the proper discipline of diet and exercise. It always boils down to the idea that we only have our lazy selves to blame if we haven't "made the most" of what we were born with, and moping about this only makes us look like poor losers.

Surveys reveal that large numbers of women are dissatisfied with their legs. Many of the faults they find with them have been given darkly humorous names — thunder thighs, chub rub, kninkles, and cankles. As I stepped deep into this topic I couldn't decide if I should laugh or cry since I, too, have always hated my legs. No way will Rod Stewart ever sing about them!

Mind the Gap

Self-loathing of thighs became a hot topic in 2012 when the concept of "thigh gap" (a space between your thighs) officially invaded women's minds after a Victoria's Secret fashion show featuring models with incredibly thin thighs. However, an isolated event did not create this mindset. Women have been bombarded with images of wafer-thin actresses with legs thinner than many women's arms for decades. It was always bad enough to see this on models, but watching these actresses on TV every week seeded the idea that there was something wrong with us if we didn't look like them. But how did they do it? Was it all thanks to surgery? Celebrities usually deny it.

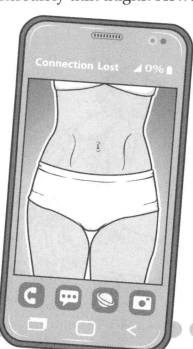

The problem is, most women do not have thigh gap, nor can they achieve it through ordinary diet and exercise. Thigh gap swept the internet with a flood of posts glorifying it. New terms popped up, such as a "Toblerone tunnel" to describe a desirable triangular gap below the crotch. The concept of "perfect legs" became more and more of a distant dream to the average woman, driving some to eating disorders in the quest to ditch those "thunder thighs" for the new elusive ideal, thigh gap.

Aye, There's the Rub, Chub

Perhaps the only good thing to come out of the thigh gap obsession was a backlash against extreme thinness. We now see a variety of body types in ads. Has this led to more "thigh acceptance"? Maybe, but only time will tell. Women had been concerned about their thighs long before thigh gap, especially during the days of the mini skirt.

If you think wearing pants is the solution, think again. Women with chafing thighs then have to deal with "noisy thigh syndrome," that swishy, swooshing, and/or squeaking sound pants make as one walks. This is related to a larger issue, "chub rub," the painful rash and bumps developed from sweat and friction when thighs in motion rub together. It can be embarrassing to be caught in the locker room applying deodorant, coconut oil, baby powder, or anti-chafing sticks down there. Worse yet, what about the awkward moment when your new significant other realizes *why* that lubricant is in the medicine cabinet!

LEGS !

YES, EVERYONE'S LOOKING AT YOUR LEGS. **WITH SKIRTS FOUR OR MORE INCHES ABOVE THE KNEES** YOU CAN'T HIDE THE TRUTH OF HOW YOUR LEGS REALLY LOOK. IF YOUR LEGS AREN'T BEAUTIFUL AND SHAPELY — DO AS THE SHOW GIRLS DO, GET THEIR FABULOUS METHOD THAT WILL SO QUICKLY PUT YOUR ENTIRE LEG LINE — YOUR THIGHS, CALFS, ANKLES AND THOSE SO IMPORTANT KNEES, INTO SHOW GIRL LOVELINESS. SEND TODAY ONLY $1. NOTHING ELSE TO BUY.

SHOW GIRL LEGS
21 West 47th Street, New York, N.Y

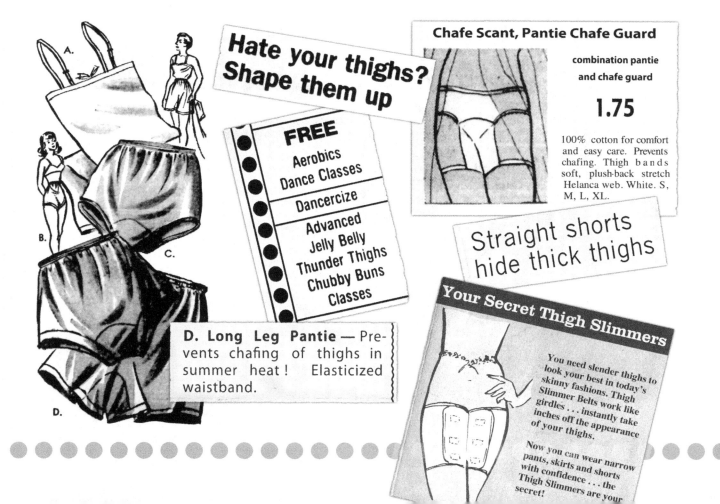

Hate your thighs? Shape them up

FREE
Aerobics
Dance Classes
Dancercize
Advanced
Jelly Belly
Thunder Thighs
Chubby Buns
Classes

D. Long Leg Pantie — Prevents chafing of thighs in summer heat! Elasticized waistband.

Chafe Scant, Pantie Chafe Guard
combination pantie and chafe guard
1.75
100% cotton for comfort and easy care. Prevents chafing. Thigh bands soft, plush-back stretch Helanca web. White. S, M, L, XL.

Straight shorts hide thick thighs

Your Secret Thigh Slimmers
You need slender thighs to look your best in today's skinny fashions. Thigh Slimmer Belts work like girdles . . . instantly take inches off the appearance of your thighs.

Now you can wear narrow pants, skirts and shorts with confidence . . . the Thigh Slimmers are your secret!

A Kninkle in Time

Whew! Enough about the thighs — let's move down to the knees. Knees, perhaps women's most hated part of the body. Ask a woman to describe them, and she may say *puffy, fat, knobby, wrinkly, saggy, dimply,* or just plain **ugly**. Rarely will she exclaim, "Why, they're beautiful!" Unless, that is, you're as fortunate as Ziegfeld dancer Ann Pennington who was acclaimed for having the "most beautiful knees in the world" in 1936.

Yep! I'm the *bee's knees!*

ANN PENNINGTON

Puffy, fat, knobby, wrinkly, saggy, and dimply are timeless complaints passed down through generations, but a relatively new term has been added to the lexicon — "kninkles," a.k.a knee wrinkles. It's interesting to note that while body acceptance has grown in the media, the harsh scrutiny of legs has gotten worse. Along with thigh gap and cankles, kninkles are something new to feel bad about.

Anybody can get kninkles. In fact, thin women who work out are particularly prone to them. The same is true for older women, even if they stayed fit their whole lives. A popular celebrity gossip topic is who has kninkles and who has had a knee lift or other procedures to remove them. Knee contouring, liposuction, laser resurfacing, and knee creams are all available — for women with enough money to foot the bill.

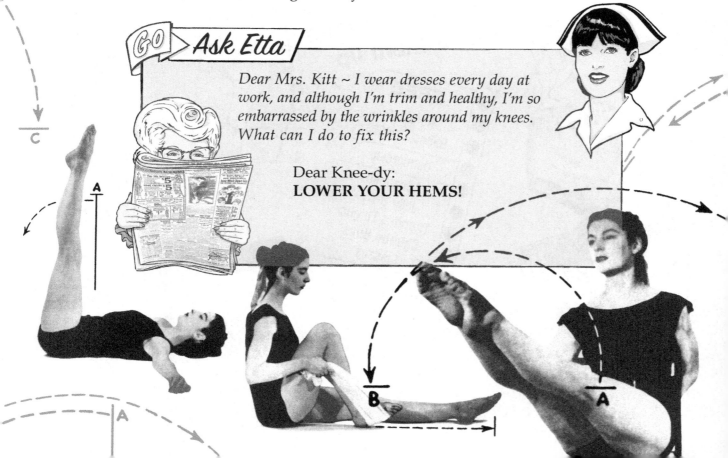

GO > Ask Etta

Dear Mrs. Kitt ~ I wear dresses every day at work, and although I'm trim and healthy, I'm so embarrassed by the wrinkles around my knees. What can I do to fix this?

Dear Knee-dy:
LOWER YOUR HEMS!

Beauty Is Only Shin Deep

The 21st century has also brought us "cankles," a mashup of "calves" and "ankles," meaning one's ankles are so thick that it looks like the calves go straight to the feet. Sometimes thick ankles are temporarily caused by pregnancy, medication, or illness. Other times, they are caused by one's weight and can be slimmed down through diet and exercise. The third scenario is that they are something you inherit, and not much can be done other than cosmetic surgery such as ankle thread lifts. These days, anything and everything on one's body can get a lift!

A lunchtime lift to trim those ankles could be a tempting alternative to exercise. In a beauty advice column from 1930, a 14-year-old girl who wanted to reduce her thick ankles was given this advice:

Walking four or five miles out of doors every day will help you to build trim ankles and calves. Practice walking on the tiptoes and do dancing steps in your bedroom every night and morning.

When will this girl have time to study? That's a lot of effort spent on one small leg part! What if she had to work on the entire leg? She would never get her homework done!

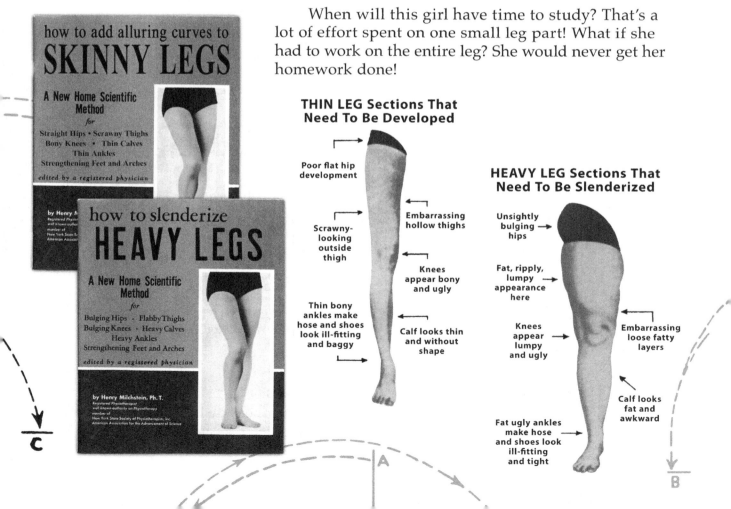

Legs Gone Wrong

"Cellulite" was a word that was once associated with hardware and insulation until 1973 when Nicole Ronsard's book *Cellulite: Those Lumps, Bumps, and Bulges You Couldn't Lose Before* became a best seller and inspired a new female obsession. Cellulite, the lumpy fatty deposits just under the skin, was described by the author as "fat gone wrong" that required a new suite of beauty regimens to combat it. Cellulite-fighting massage, creams, wraps, and diets sprung up in the market, and women have been self-conscious about "cottage cheese" legs ever since.

Another source of female frustration is varicose veins. Women are prone to them thanks in part to the abundance of the hormone progesterone. Women might develop them during pregnancy or after 40 (the magical age when everything starts to go wrong), but varicose veins can appear at any time. A variety of treatments are available, but they are still one more thing standing in the way of song-worthy legs. All through my childhood I saw ads in magazines for treating or hiding varicose veins, and they sure looked scary! Back in the day, women didn't typically wear pants, so there was no way to easily hide these pesky veins unless you sent away for a miracle cure in the back pages of a magazine, where all scientific breakthroughs apparently could be found!

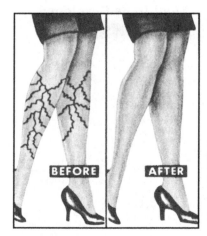

If the Shoe Doesn't Fit —Wear It!

We're finally down to the topic of feet. What about them? Well, what if they are — *ahem* — on the large side? The average size of women's feet has increased over the years, yet a stigma lingers that a woman should have small dainty feet. This notion dates back to the practice of foot binding in China and has never completely left.

Surveys show that most women buy shoes that are too small. Why? Denial as we grow older and our feet spread. A refusal to trudge to the far end of the shoe racks at the store. A dread of having to special order one's shoes. Where's the fun in shoe shopping if you have to ask the clerk if your size can be trucked in before the dance?

With a few exceptions, shoes are marketed for style. They can also be status symbols. In certain circles, a lot can be riding on one's choice of shoes. So, what happens when you're a "shoe dropout" like me who has adopted sneakers as my daily shoe? At this point, I can barely hobble around in a pair of heels for more than an hour, so I have to devise a "funky" fashion statement that involves flat-heel boots. Oh, to have been alive in 1917 when army boots were in fashion!

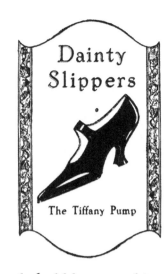

Dainty Slippers

The Tiffany Pump

Strutting through life in too-small shoes with stylish heels and pointy toes can lead to painful foot problems such as corns and calluses that ironically make feet less beautiful. What's the solution? Heck if I know. The choice of shoes and the amount of pain we are willing to take with them is a personal one. Who are we to judge unless we walk a mile in each other's shoes?

Fresh, flattering and frankly feminine

The Last Resort

Not every woman can become a "movie star beauty." Nor do we all want to be. So, what is left for those who aren't if they want to level the playing field? The answer can be found in a host of books, articles, and how-to programs touting the benefits of poise and charm over beauty of the "skin deep" variety. They focus on two key points. First, every woman has something special to offer — *if* she knows how to apply herself. Second, even the loveliest woman sullies her beauty when she indulges in uncouth behavior.

This form of "self-improvement" involves a lot of reading up on the rules of etiquette along with a disciplined lifestyle that develops both the body and mind. A typical list of attributes that the poised and charming woman must develop includes:

- A relaxed, lithe body developed through daily exercise.
- A glowing complexion as a result of a healthy diet and skin care regimens.
- A poised nobility expressed through perfect posture and impeccable grooming.
- A bright personality enhanced by regular reading and sensible sleep.
- A graceful presence embodied by moving like a lady and standing like a model.
- A flair for fashion appropriate for one's age, body type, and the occasion.
- A knack for enchanting conversation, which means speaking clearly, in pleasant tones, with utmost sincerity — *and* listening more than gabbing away!
- A reputation as the consummate hostess who practices the fine art of hospitality through tasteful interior decorating, gourmet cooking, and flawless manners.

In short? ***Be yourself!***

BE YOUR *ALLURING* SELF!
You can become Fascinating and Glamorous, too!

Don't stand on the sidelines and let other girls have all the fun!

Excuses, Excuses

When you consider that all it takes is one good mail away how-to manual and a resolve to follow its guidance to the letter, what excuse do any of us have for not giving ourselves a little polish? Well, what if you're already exhausted from all those bust development and tummy trimming exercises? What if you've spent all your spare time dancing on tiptoes to reduce those cankles? Or what if you have a doctor's note to excuse you? That trumps everything, right?

Think again. You have **no excuse** for depriving yourself from a life of glamour! Just take your daily iron! Mother warned you…
but did you listen?

BORDERLINE ANEMIA*
can deprive a girl of glamour . . . and dates!

Medical Science says:
Thousands who have pale faces—whose strength is at low ebb—may have a blood deficiency

ROUND SHOULDERS SLOUCH?
Gone with
"Posture Queen"

What about the women toiling at work for long hours, too spent to follow through with the daily calisthenics required for a graceful presence and model's stance? No excuse! If you're drooping, just prop yourself up with an industrial strength bra, and you can be transformed from sad case to beauty queen.

Besides, nobody's saying that a woman can't rest her feet from time to time. In fact, many charm experts advise that the truly poised woman never rushes into anything and budgets her energy so that she can always be ready whenever poise and charm are needed — *which is **always!***

Take it easy, sister. Rushing means a much too early old age.

Since rushing will only lead me to an early grave, may I interrupt for a moment? This appearance of the Posture Queen is my last opportunity to hail this model as the Queen of the Mail Away Beauty Ads. She pops up multiple times in almost any movie magazine from the late 1960s–early 70s. An unsung icon of poise and charm!

What's Wrong Here?

"I AM SORRY TO INTERRUPT BUT—"

Never interrupt a conversation.

Uh-oh… I have just been notified that interrupting is a no-no. Where was I? Oh! About to discuss how the exhausted woman can still maintain her poise and charm…

REMOVE UNWANTED HAIR FOREVER with Permagon

ONLY $7.95

No smelly chemicals— No painful tweezing. A few easy minutes and ugly unwanted hairs are out and good.

SLIM-A WAIST

WAIST-CINCHER BRA FRONT OPENING

only $2.98

GLORIOUS YOUNG CURVES FOR THE FULLER FIGURE

SATISFACTION GUARANTEED OR YOUR MONEY BACK

Have You Tried Speed?

Let's face it, even if your Posture Queen industrial strength bra has propped you up, you still might lack the pep required for that bright personality in the vivacious woman.

The guidebooks tell you to get regular sleep and not stay out late at night burning the candle at both ends. However, they seem to be overlooking those matters of raising kids and taking care of the house while possibly also holding down a job or even multiple jobs. As they say in song, women do get weary.

How to get that perky Laura Petrie charm? One solution popular in the 1960s was over-the-counter stimulants. Ads promised women that they could be transformed from "the droopiest wallflower — pining for a single admiring glance… a little attention… even a kind word" to a one-woman pep squad with a "sparkling smile that scintillates with her newly-found energy… a great big, economy-size 'man-trap' smile that completely devastates all the men!" Wow! Now the only question is *how am I going to find the energy to run to the store?*

If popping pills was the answer for a young fading wallflower like Lola, it would likely become a lifetime habit. Advertisers have warned women of the dangers of getting sloppy as they age. Vivacious charm is a lifetime commitment, ladies! Curb those little idiosyncrasies — *nobody likes them!* (Note: I am doomed.)

**WHATEVER LOLA WANTS…
LOLA GETS…**

*and YOU can
have it TOO!*

ENERGEX IS GUARANTEED TO PLEASE—you test it at OUR EXPENSE! if you are not fully convinced, within 10 days, that ENERGEX has helped you — then return the remaining tablets for a FULL REFUND of your money.

**MAIL
THIS
QUICK
ENERGY
COUPON
NOW!**

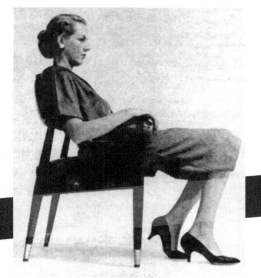

DON'T SLUMP in your chair when you sit. That's a postion reserved for teen-agers only—and nobody's going to mistake you for a teen-ager.

Ten rules to take 10 years off your appearance.

1. Maintain an erect posture.
2. Stand firmly on your feet.
3. Put youth in your stride.
4. Sit down briskly.
5. Guard against slumping.
6. Get up with agility.
7. Make your voice vital.
8. Make your gestures definite.
9. Cultivate a bright face.
10. Curb those little idiosyncrasies.

It's Not Them, It's You

The fine art of mastering finishing school takes on a new challenge during "that time of the month." If ever there were a time when a woman should be allowed to crawl into a fetal ball, feast on chocolate, and lash out at anyone who asks too much of her… it's "that time."

PMS, short for Pre-Menstrual Syndrome, Psychotic Mood Swings, Pack My Stuff, Perpetual Munching Spree, Pardon My Shriek, or Pass My Sweats, is a problem that is still under debate as to whether it's a real consequence of hormonal imbalance or merely something in women's heads.

Ask any person who has lived with a menstruating woman, and he or she will probably say, "I'm a believer!" Whether a woman is on edge from PMS or suffering excruciating pain from cramps during her period, she might not be putting charm and poise at the top of her priority list.

I used to suffer from menstrual cramps.

"Now I'm Full of Pep"

"HOUSEWORK IS FUN"

says Gloria Adams after taking Lydia E. Pinkham's Vegetable Compound

Housewife tells how this famous medicine gave her new strength

CHECK YOUR FAULTS

Ask your family or friends whether or not you show any of these symptoms.

Are you cross? .... ☐
Are you nervous? .... ☐
Are you run-down? .... ☐
Are you always tired?. .... ☐
Are you ever hysterical? ...... ☐
Are you ever blue? .... ☐
Do you ever feel faint? .... ☐
Are you ever dizzy? .... ☐
Are you "all in"? .... ☐

If you have one or more of these symptoms and they are

However, advertisers have been quick to point out that any bad behavior during this time is solely the woman's responsibility and that she ought to buy a remedy that will bring back her inner Jekyll that everybody knows and loves and defeat that hormonal Hyde.

Early remedies such as Lydia Pinkham's Vegetable Compound promised to free women of the misery of "female complaints." Making its debut in the mid-1800s, this compound was dismissed as quackery by the government, partly due to the high alcohol content in the formula, but some of the herbs in it are still used to relieve these problems. Hey, anything that makes housework fun sounds more than a bit intriguing to me!

In the early part of the 20th century, Chichester's Pills were another remedy that women could reach for to "help relieve those 'anti-social' symptomatic jumpy nerves." After a seven-year legal battle with the government, the Supreme Court ruled that their claims were false and fraudulent.

Products have come and gone over the decades, many of which advertise to girls who have just reached puberty. The relationship between popularity and menstrual management has been drilled into girls' minds as soon as they get "the curse."

Even if a girl is able to maintain a sunny disposition, there's that side issue of water weight. So much to deal with while facing the larger issues of life. *Smile, girls, smile! I wonder… might cramps be the untold secret behind Mona Lisa's enigmatic smile?*

Girls!
Do you suffer from
nervous tension
On "CERTAIN DAYS" of the month?

YOU'RE GROWN UP WHEN

it's not baby fat,
it's water-weight build-up.

Unfortunately, during the week before your menstrual period, your body accumulates fluids. This temporary water-weight gain can make you feel puffy, "full," and uncomfortable (which in turn makes you irritable, crampy…simply "gross").

Of course, if you still look puffy after taking PAMPRIN, maybe it _is_ fat, Baby.

Prevent "vacation drag" with Tampax tampons

Make it a real vacation if you take a vacation this fall. Don't miss 5 days of fun just because it's "that time of the month." With Tampax tampons you'll be comple…

Peggy's BRIGHT WITH **MIDOL**

Midol

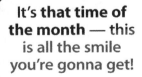

It's **that time of the month** — this is all the smile you're gonna get!

Pre-Menstrual Tension and Depression Are _Not_ Just A Woman's Imagination!

Aging Gracefully

Why Women Grow Old More Quickly Than Men

Greater Percentage of Anaemia—Lack of Iron in the Blood—Among Women Makes Them Lose Much of Their Youth, Beauty and Former Attractiveness And Become Fretful, Nervous and Run Down

At 20 Years

At 30 Years

At 40 Years

So, in case you didn't know, because I did not until I started researching, there's this thing in advertising about women growing older more quickly than men. *Eek!* I thought the urban legend told that men simply had an edge because they grew dashing and debonair as they aged — *not* because women were being sucked through a time-space accelerator that caused freakishly rapid aging. You learn something new every day.

Why is it that aging for women is continually portrayed as worse than death? Why must we throw out the old face for a new one at some point in our lives? The answer is obvious — to keep us buying more products and services, usually at a high price. Why? To not lose all our investment in time, energy, and money over the years to "better" ourselves… to preserve that vivacious edge. When does the chase after the mirage of perfection end? *Never!* In her later years, my mother would not walk with a cane because "it made her look old." *She was 90!*

HORRIFYING QUOTE ABOUT AGING

Do you see why a woman starts aging from her head down?

There's many a young body carrying around an old head. You must learn to give face, neck, and shoulders more circulation. Lean an ironing board against a low bed, put pillows under buttocks and heels on wall. Work up to a half hour a day. Do it daily. Relax. Think of nothing except to count your blessings.

~1930s hair color ad

A NEW FACE
—A NEW FUTURE!

How Plastic Surgery easily takes years off the prematurely aged face, quickly reshapes an ugly nose and corrects other facial blemishes is told and illustrated with 88 before-and-after pictures in fascinating book, YOUR NEW FACE IS YOUR FORTUNE, written by famous Plastic Surgeon. Yours, post-paid in plain wrapper—only **25c**

FRANKLIN HOUSE *Publishers*
629 Drexel Bldg. Philadelphia, Pa. Dept. 11-R

GO Ask Etta

Dear Mrs. Kitt ~ I have always been well-regarded for my style, manners, and sharp wit. Oddly, now that I'm growing older (and wiser), young people laugh in my face when I correct them and say I'm "outdated." How do I gracefully respond to this?

~ Golden Oldie

Dear Oldie: The mark of a true lady is to never stoop to another person's level, no matter how rude he or she may be. Bite your tongue and turn the other cheek. Then have a glass of wine. On me.

❀ THINGS NOT TO DO TODAY ❀

Don't look at your feet. Don't act as if you were studying the pavement.

MUCH BETTER!

Keep The Nag Out Of Your Voice

NAGGING HEADS the list of qualities husbands with a whining, complaining voice winds up

Don't Lounge Over The Table

Poised Woman Holds Herself With Dignity.

Poised Woman Does Not Fuss With Clothes

"Would you please tell that friend of yours," said a man to his wife, "to stop her shenanigans. She makes me nervous."

"You tell her," resp...

"I embarrassed my husband every time I opened my mouth"

DON'T GIVE WAY TO THE NERVES

A Calm, Evenly Poised Woman Is a Blessing in the Home.

SHOPPING LIST
- Plain Yogurt
- Cottage Cheese
- Gum
- Grapefruit
- Bran Fiber
- Celery
- Cabbage
- Diet Soda
- Fat Free Cookies

A really smart woman never is a table lounger.

You know how the most beautiful woman can lose her charming hold over folks and come down to the ordinary level with a dull thud by the little things she does. Well, table lounging is one of these little things!

Real poise makes you eas... pleasantly at home at th...

Never, never chew gum, which is about as ill-mannered as spitting on the streets. It toughens your jaw line and gives the impression of a cow at leisure just before milking time.

Another r...

DON'T laugh too much.

KEEP UP THE Good Work!

6. Don't stuff food in your mouth with both hands at once.

DON'T WALK TOO SLOW
DON'T WALK TOO FAST

DON'T make yourself cheap.

DON'T talk too much.

Problem is PIMPLES and You ing THIS... for Pete's Sake...

ASHAMED OF YOUR BOSOM?

CHECK YOUR FAULTS
Ask your family or friends whether or not you show any of these symptoms.

HATE YOUR HAIR?

THE END IS IN SIGHT

Hindsight

As we come to the final stop on our journey, we must confront the thing that ironically is so hard for us to see, the gluteus maximus, the largest muscle in our bodies.

One's backside is a lot like the dark side of the moon. We know it's there, but it's hard to see without assistance. This is one aspect of beauty that puts us at a disadvantage with anybody we encounter. Everything else is easy to check and primp to our satisfaction before leaving the house. With the rear, we spend our lives checking it out in the mirror and asking others how it looks.

The size and shape of one's buttocks is one of "Mother Nature's surprises" that comes about with puberty. We don't get a lot of choice in the matter. Then, other factors such as pregnancy, lifestyle, and aging continue to mess with it, creating another lifelong responsibility for us to manage. Unfortunately, rear ends tend to have a will of their own, not always cooperating with our plans and dreams for them.

As with everything else, women are conditioned to want whatever it is they don't have. Adding to this are the fickle trends of fashion, which have caused women to shift from the question *"Does this make my butt look* **big***?"* to *"How do I make my butt look* **bigger***?"*

To this, I raise the philosophical question, *is there really such a thing as a bad ass?* Admittedly, this part of the body is the first to be insulted in a heated fight, leaving us vulnerable, but as I look at couples happily walking hand in hand down the street I see derrieres of all shapes and sizes. Are there any deal breakers when you're with the right person? Yet, since the 1990s, the decade *Rolling Stone* magazine dubbed the "Decade of the Butt," no other body part has been so celebrated, scrutinized, and hailed as the living end. Brazilian butt lifts, silicone implants, hydrogel injections, padded panties, butt-buster workouts, and tush-lifting jeans are just some of the options available to women striving to get the *maximus* out of their *gluteus*.

Gibson Girl, Hourglass Figure Due for Revival

It's easy to trace this trend back to the late 1990s when Jennifer Lopez became a star. It is said she was the inspiration for the 1992 Sir Mix-A-Lot hit song, "Baby Got Back," one in a wave of hit songs in the 2000s that focused keenly on women's backsides. Then, in 2014 Kim Kardashian bared her ample behind on the cover of *Paper* and "broke the internet" as it caused a media sensation.

However, dressing to show off one's rear dates back much farther, to the Victorian era 1800s with corsets and bustles designed to create a "wasp waist" and hourglass figure. This led to the less exaggerated but still curvy Gibson Girl style of the early 20th century, as idealized by illustrator Charles Dana Gibson. The Gibson Girl was tall and slender with a tiny waist, large bust, and wide hips… a silhouette made possible by cinching the waist with corsets. Women were covered up, but the cinched waist conjured curvy sex appeal.

Nice butt!

Although the Gibson Girl look was natural compared to the Victorian wasp waist and bustle, it was still an unrealistic body image and reserved for high society. When I was growing up in the 70s, I never thought the natural look would go away, but corsets and the hourglass figure have revivals from time to time, one of those times being now. This is unfortunate for me because I am shaped like a fire hydrant, not an hourglass. I would have to wear huge platform shoes and a corset to even begin to approach the Gibson Girl look, and I would probably pass out and topple off a curb if I even attempted it. I also don't measure up to modern standards of endowment in my behind, so what am I to do? 500 squats daily?

Expert Advice

My secret to a toned behind? Always take the stairs instead of the elevator.
And work on the 40th floor!

Don't Be Sad — Pad!

INSTANT CURVES
TO FILL YOUR DESIGNER JEANS!

"Bottom Secret" Padded Panties round you where you're not — and never tell a soul!

STYLE A: Padded only in back to curve you deliciously

STYLE B: Padded sides and back to round you ravishingly

CONTROLS STOMACH — SUPPORTS BACK — FILLS YOU OUT WHERE NATURE LET YOU DOWN!

MAIL NO-RISK COUPON TODAY

Considering that the size of one's rear goes in and out of fashion, perhaps it makes sense to skip the squats and simply add padding the same way we can with our bras. After all, the Gibson Girl went out of vogue and was replaced by the flappers in the 1920s. Women tossed their corsets, wrapped their bosoms to flatten them, and wore short skirts to create a lean line. Since then, fashions have come and gone, keeping generations of women busy trying to find a way for their fannies to look great in whatever's new.

Many or most of us have struggled to squeeze into a tight pair of jeans or a sexy wiggle dress, but what about the case of adding something extra without splurging on a bustle? Designer Emilio Pucci designed the "Uplift Viva" panty girdle in 1957 ostensibly because he thought a flat behind was an unspeakable horror. Frederick Mellinger who founded Frederick's of Hollywood in 1947 also saw a market for this, so he hired a sculptor to do a bust of the perfect buttocks and used a mold to replicate it for his "Living End" girdle. Now any woman could have a *callipygian* figure, meaning "having a shapely rear end." *Just pick one up at the store!*

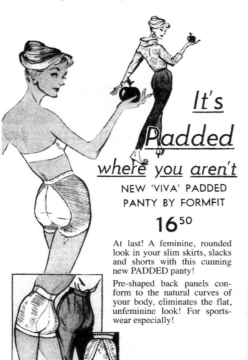

It's **Padded** *where you aren't*

NEW 'VIVA' PADDED PANTY BY FORMFIT

16⁵⁰

At last! A feminine, rounded look in your slim skirts, slacks and shorts with this cunning new PADDED panty!

Pre-shaped back panels conform to the natural curves of your body, eliminates the flat, unfeminine look! For sportswear especially!

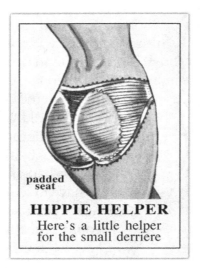

padded seat

HIPPIE HELPER
Here's a little helper for the small derriere

Add more "wow" to your wiggle with the new Nemo padded panty girdle
If your figure isn't all that it should be, improve upon nature with Fanny Falsies, the new Nemo padded panty girdles that give alluring curves to the unfortunately flat.

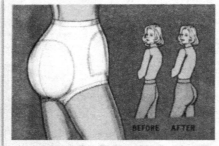

BEFORE   AFTER

ADD INSTANT CURVES TO YOUR FIGURE with Padded Panty! Be a shapelier YOU—with glamorous, provocative curves you never dreamed you'd have! Pretty panty is smoothly, secretly padded to fill you out in all the right places! Gives you an alluring new silhouette in clingy knits, pants —everything you wear!

In the end, though, what happens when the clothes come off? The freewheeling 60s and 70s had a "take it all off" mentality, and even if you weren't taking it all off, the clothing you kept on often left little to the imagination. The beautiful behind also began to be officially celebrated in the media with Britain's Rear of the Year award making its debut in 1976 (bestowing the award to Dame Barbara Windsor of the *Carry On* film series fame). The pressure was on for women to get their rears in gear. But what of the woman with "something extra" that she didn't love and couldn't hide? Would she be negatively judged? Care to guess? Read on.

The Dreadful Spread

HIP REDUCING ROUTINES
You can diet until you become feather-light and still be hip-heavy. Reduction in the hipline is assured only by exercise.

The increase of women working office jobs in the 1950s brought them something new to dread, a thing called "secretary spread." The idea behind it is that sitting all day will cause one's lovely behind to lose tone and spread out wide. That is, unless one takes measures to counteract this dark force, e.g. good posture, elastic undergarments to keep everything where it should be, and, of course — exercise! Yay! Yet another workout regimen! Let's see… when should I fit this one in? After my bust development arm circles or after my knee lift?

The computer age has blown this issue much larger, well beyond of the confines of the secretarial arts. Many women do their work seated all day. Have a desk job? No matter how fulfilling or important it may be, it makes a woman guilty of being sedentary. Unless she carves out the time to hit the gym after work, she is not living up to expectations for charming womanhood. *(Note: It appears that somehow men are immune to this.)*

As an article from 1969 explains:

Get Hep If Hips Spread, Rock And Roll Fat Off

Fight hip spread

Pleats Will Disguise Secretarial Spread

Too Much Hip?
THE SECRETARY'S SPREAD afflicts as many women as the common cold with equally unglamorous results. Though there are no miracle drugs for either affliction, here's an exercise that will help

You don't need to be a detective to solve the mystery of "the missing figure." A torso that misses being shapely is usually a case of neglect. Most often that neglected area is the waist down! Part of the problem undoubtedly is the occupational hazard experienced by many "sedentary" young women — it includes sitting too long at the table, too!

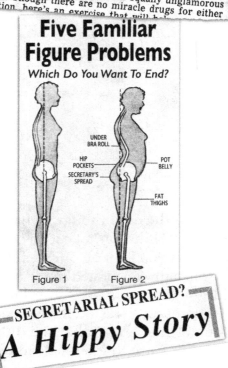

Five Familiar Figure Problems
Which Do You Want To End?

UNDER BRA ROLL

HIP POCKETS

SECRETARY'S SPREAD

POT BELLY

FAT THIGHS

Figure 1   Figure 2

Memo: Buy pleated skirt.

SECRETARIAL SPREAD?
A Hippy Story

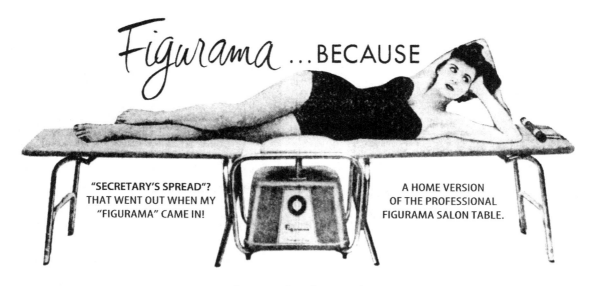

Figurama ...BECAUSE

"SECRETARY'S SPREAD"? THAT WENT OUT WHEN MY "FIGURAMA" CAME IN!

A HOME VERSION OF THE PROFESSIONAL FIGURAMA SALON TABLE.

The Naked Truth

Miss Universe of 1958 sported a figure that measured 36-24-36, and for decades afterward, these measurements have been popularly cited as the proportions of the perfect woman. This closely correlates to the "Rule of Ten" from the 1950s–60s which states that one's bustline and hips should have the same measurements and the waist ten inches smaller. How do you measure up? I'm not feeling so hot.

The good news is (I suppose) is that no matter how one's bottom measures up, all is forgiven as long as we keep it **toned**. Once upon a time, women scrambled in spring to get it in shape for summer when the swimsuits come out and one must reveal the nearly naked truth.

Well-toned buttocks critical

Unfortunately, these days more and more fashions all year round reveal all. Yoga pants and thong sportswear, swimwear, and underwear have left women with nowhere to hide. So, is it any wonder that women are preoccupied with bringing up the rear? It's no surprise that butt lifts are in and corsets are back!

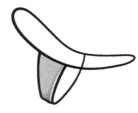

for a Smoother Line

start with

Skintees

... the rayon knit **panty**
that fits like your skin!

The Shame of Panty Lines

In closing, I must not overlook the horror of panty lines. The term "panty lines" emerged in 1975 with the release of the Playtex Free Spirit Pantsliner, a Spanx-like undergarment that smoothed bulges and "ugly panty lines" on women wearing clingy slacks. This was the heyday of nylon and polyester clothing. Just add a heater pumping away in the office on a winter's day, and women found themselves victim to the embarrassment of static cling.

Playtex had obviously hit upon a profitable new market, for soon after, panty line-fighting products such as Underalls, Slenderalls, and Undie-L'eggs hit the market, and women have been worried about panty lines ever since. What if *(shudder)* somebody detects them?

Thong underwear is another way to vanquish ugly panty lines — remove the panties and you have no lines! Another option is to wear heavy wool clothing all year round. As for me, I just stay home and sit in front of the computer. While I'm at it, I think I'll write a book.

And with that, my friends, we come to the end of the **end!**

You could look better in pants than ever before!

Just slip on a new Free Spirit Pantsliner...

What you want is a beautifully smooth natural look in pants.
And that's what the Free Spirit® Pantsliner from Playtex® gives you.
Because it smooths out ugly panty lines and that pudge from panty elastic.
The hidden tummy panel flattens your tummy, too!
We made it with a delightful, soft, lightweight material with "no-show" seams.
It's the smooth way to look smoother in pants!

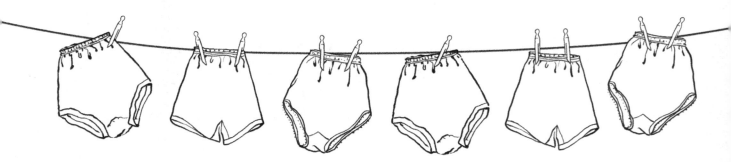

THE END

But,
How Are We Doing Now?

High Self-Esteem

If you read this book all the way up to here and you're still with me, congratulations. How are you feeling about yourself? Are you feeling a little bit *used?*

I am pleased to report that I emerged from my deep dive into the dark trenches of women's advertising feeling not worse, but in fact, **better** about myself. All these messages bombarding me with who I must be, how I must look, and how I'm in need of constant improvement have lost their power. Now, when I see one of these messages in my daily life, I laugh and think *"Oh, there's **that** again!"*

How are you doing? Measure your self-esteem by rating how you agree or disagree with the following statements. If you are writing down 1's and 2's — read this guide again!

Self-Esteem Post-Survey	Strongly Disagree 1	Disagree 2	Neutral 3	Agree 4	Strongly Agree 5
Describe my bustline...? Sure — *Nice rack!*					
My face is awesome. I look just like me!					
If you can't live with my B.O., you know where you can go.					
Call me "Fat." Call me "Skinny." I can't hear you — *jerk!*					
Judge my hands by what they can do — not by how they look.					
Growing old sure beats the alternatives!					
My *derriere* is end-dear-ing!					

Ask Etta

Dear Mrs. Kitt ~ All us readers got together last weekend, and you know what we realized? We're just fine! People like YOU are the problem! **What do you say about that!**

Signed,
The Angry Mob

No comment.

Have We Learned Anything Now?

I don't know about you, but what I have learned is that while we have all been conditioned to strive for perfection... **nobody's perfect.**

ahem...

MISS NANA STERLING
"America's most perfect woman."
1916

Made in United States
North Haven, CT
03 January 2022

14161991R00063